Sell It on eBay:

A Guide to Successful Online Auctions

Second Edition

By Jim Heid and Toby Malina

Peachpit
Press

Sell It on eBay: A Guide to Successful Online Auctions
Second Edition
Jim Heid and Toby Malina

Peachpit Press
1249 Eighth Street
Berkeley, CA 94710
510/524-2178
800/283-9444
510/524-2221 (fax)

Find us on the Web at www.peachpit.com
To report errors, please send a note to errata@peachpit.com
Peachpit Press is a division of Pearson Education
Copyright © 2006 by Jim Heid and Toby Malina

Editor: Barbara Assadi, BayCreative
Art Direction/Illustration: Arne Hurty, BayCreative
Compositor: Jonathan Woolson, thinkplaydesign
Production Coordinator: Pat Christenson
Indexer: Emily Glossbrenner, FireCrystal Communications
Cover Design: Arne Hurty, BayCreative

ISBN 0-321-35680-2
9 8 7 6 5 4 3 2 1
Printed and bound in the United States of America

For Maryellen

For Jess

About the Authors

Jim Heid has been working with and writing about personal computers since 1980, when he computerized his home-built ham radio station with a Radio Shack TRS-80 Model I. He has been writing for *Macworld* magazine since 1984, and has written over a dozen computer books, including the bestselling *The Macintosh iLife* series, from Peachpit Press and Avondale Media. He has also written for *PC World*, *Internet World*, and *Newsweek* magazines as well as the *Los Angeles Times*.

Jim was smitten by World Wide Web in 1996. One year later, he dragged his wife and dog on a seven-week, 10,000-mile road trip to research and write about the Internet's impact on rural America, a trip that was covered by *USA Today*, the *New York Times*, and *MSNBC*.

Although Jim advocates a very basic design approach to eBay listings, he is no stranger to the fancier side of Web site design. Since 1998, he has served as Conference Chair for the acclaimed Web Design series of conferences produced by Thunder Lizard Productions. He has helped to produce dozens of Web conferences and has spoken to thousands of Web professionals on the subjects of usability and digital media.

Jim lives with his standard poodle and mascot, Sophie, on a windswept headland near Mendocino, California.

Toby Malina has spent nearly twenty years working as a technical consultant in the computer field. In 1995, she joined Thunder Lizard Productions, a Seattle-based conference production company, as Technical/Editorial Director.

The principal of MacDaddy Consulting, Toby works with a number of companies as, among other things, technical director, producer, and editor. In addition to her continuing relationship with Thunder Lizard, she works as senior field technician for One World Journeys, creators of online wilderness expeditions and outdoor adventures dedicated to environmental awareness and education. She is a coauthor of the three-volume *Web Site Graphics* series and works as a technical/copy editor for a diverse array of publishers.

Toby became an enthusiastic eBay member on her brother's birthday in 1998. As an accumulator of computer gear and a serial shopper, she found eBay the perfect milieu to feed her cycle of shopping: buy a must-have item, get tired of it, sell it, buy something else! Having sold everything from a handful of keys thrown on a scanner bed to computer systems, she has learned many of the key tips and tricks for using eBay to make money, have fun, and keep on shopping.

In 2002, with partner Steve Broback, Toby and Jim co-founded Avondale Media, a production company focusing on instructional DVDs, seminars, and conferences.

Acknowledgements

If you've thumbed through these pages, you've seen that this is not an ordinary-looking computer book. Its extraordinary look comes from the marvelous mind of Arne Hurty, of San Francisco's BayCreative. You, sir, have done it again.

Alongside every great art director is a great editor, and that's where BayCreative's Barbara Assadi comes in. Thank you for reading and refining every word.

Then there's the man who moved the words from pixels to paper and arranged them with an artist's eye and a surgeon's attention to detail. Jonathan Woolson combines technical, design, and production mastery like no one we have ever met.

When you're pawing through the index looking for that one nugget of information, join us in thanking Emily Glossbrenner.

Thanks also go to everyone at Peachpit Press, especially Marjorie Baer, Alison Kelley, Scott Cowlin, Kim Becker, Nancy Ruenzel, and Rebecca Ross. We couldn't imagine publishing with anyone else.

We also thank our friend and Avondale Media partner Steve Broback, whose i3Forum provided the fertile soil where this book germinated.

And finally, each of us would like to offer some personal acknowledgments.

From Jim. When I began this project, I'd been using eBay for several years but didn't appreciate the nuances of selling. My mentor was Toby Malina, my friend, coauthor, and partner in crimes of all kinds. Throughout this project, you've shown talent, determination, and (once again) grace under a pressure that no one should have to endure. I couldn't have survived 2005 without you. Thank you for being there for all three of us. Next stop: the pages of *Craze*.

My love and a big hug also go to my mom, Margaret Heid, who's always there, always smiling, and always loving. My love and thanks also to Judy, Terry, Robin, Bruce, Fal, Pierre, Laura, Mimi, Violet, Coco—and Sophie, who helps me through the darkest forests.

And to Maryellen Kelly: You gave me my life. I will cherish our love forever.

From Toby. It isn't particularly unusual to find oneself in the company of a talented colleague or to make a close friend, but to find a brilliant confluence of the two is special indeed. Jim—master wordsmith, prolific author, and all-around mensch—you are the soul of devotion. I've got your back. This Fribble's for you.

I can't express adequately my deep thanks, love, and gratitude to Maryellen Kelly. You taught me so much: to embrace who I am, where I am, and the grand and lovely people around me. You gave me a lifetime of friendship in a few short years. I miss you.

To Fal, an eBay inspiration, thank you for taking care of me as we coaxed these pages along. 我愛你. 我想你.

My love and thanks to my parents, who have always found my convoluted "career" charming rather than alarming; my sister Nicole, and brother Joshua, for always being only ten digits away; and to the dames in my life, Marci, Dalin, Denise, and Coco. You give me strength.

Table of Contents

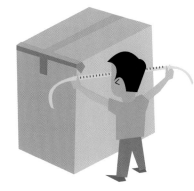

Read Me First

Welcome to **Sell It On eBay: A Guide to Successful Online Auctions, Second Edition.** Before we begin our trip, here's a roadmap of our route and some sightseeing suggestions.

Chapter 1: eBay Basics sets the stage with a look at the remarkable world of online auctions and what it takes to be a successful seller. If you haven't yet registered on eBay or created a seller's account, we'll show you how.

Chapter 2: Creating an Auction is a hands-on look at the steps involved in creating an eBay auction. At times, we'll also step back for a look at auction strategies, such as deciding what payment options you'd like to give your buyers.

Chapter 3: The Pictures describes how to take pictures that will make your items look their best, and how to refine and prepare those pictures for eBay.

Chapter 4: Text and Formatting discusses the art of eBay writing: how to prepare a title and description that will snag shoppers and inspire them to bid.

Chapter 5: Managing Your Auctions shows how to keep your auctions running smoothly by answering questions, managing bidders, and more.

Chapter 6: Sold! delves into all the details you'll need to know after your auction ends, from packing and shipping to getting paid to solving problems.

Chapter 7: The Next Step examines some options you may want to consider as your eBay sales career takes off.

And finally, some appendices provide an at-a-glance reference to all the icons and symbols you see on eBay and to common auction abbreviations and terms. We wrap up with a preview of some forthcoming—and significant—eBay selling enhancements.

A Note About eBay Motors and Real Estate Auctions

We don't cover the process of creating auctions for eBay Motors or for real estate. These are growing parts of the eBay world, but they're also very specialized types of auctions, with their own unique considerations and procedures. Many of the basic concepts we cover in this book also apply to eBay Motors and real estate auctions, but we don't dive into the specific steps.

What's New in the Second Edition—and Online

Since the first edition of this book appeared in 2003, eBay has added numerous features to its site. For example, a greatly enhanced My eBay area makes it easier to track and manage your eBay activities, and a new eBay Toolbar helps protect against cyber-crooks. eBay has also refined aspects of the auction process, such as managing shipments, dealing with bidders who don't pay, and negotiating happy endings to feedback wars.

We cover these and many more eBay enhancements in this revised edition, and we provide a sneak peek at a new method of creating auctions that's currently in development. And because the eBay scene is always evolving, we've launched a companion Web site, www.ebaymatters.com, where you'll find even more updates and news on all eBay matters. We hope you'll visit!

CHAPTER 1

eBay Basics

Introduction

Sell it on eBay. It's a simple phrase, but it has plowed its way into our cultural vocabulary. People say it in all seriousness. They say it as a joke. They say it all the time.

That CD player you don't use any more? Sell it on eBay. That blouse that seems to have, ahem, shrunk over the years? Sell it on eBay. The toy train set collecting dust in the attic? Sell it on eBay.

Sell it on eBay. It's a simple phrase, but it describes a process that isn't always simple. A successful online auction is a rich recipe. Start with equal parts of good market research, good writing, and good photography. Mix well, then bake for up to ten days in a vast, often complex Web site. Serve with generous helpings of honesty, courtesy, and customer service.

Cooking isn't difficult when you have good directions, and that's where we come in. We've taken the steps behind creating eBay auctions and presented them in a concise, easy-to-read format.

The world is full of eBay hype: Get rich on eBay! Quit your job! We won't insult your intelligence with that sort of thing. Yes, there are people who close their retail stores in favor of selling on eBay. Maybe you'll join them. Yes, there are PowerSellers who rake in thousands of dollars a month. Maybe you'll become one.

Or maybe you'll join us and the millions of other people who create an auction now and then—to make a few extra bucks, to unclutter a closet, or just to have fun.

Ready to sell it on eBay? Let's learn how.

The first documented auctions occurred in the Babylonian Empire about 500 B.C. Often called *wedding auctions,* they involved the sale of women to the highest bidders. This dark side of auction history (and there are many) is chillingly depicted in an 1875 painting, *The Marriage Market Babylon,* by Edwin Long.

Roman treasurers would often auction plundered booty. A spear was driven into the ground to mark the location and beginning of the auction. These auctions were said to take place *sub hasta,* or "under the spear." The Italian word for auction, *asta,* traces its roots to this.

In 193 A.D., the entire Roman Empire was sold at auction. After the current emperor was assassinated, the Praetorian Guard auctioned the empire to the highest bidder, Didius Julianus. He reigned for sixty-six days before being executed (see "winner's curse" on opposite page).

In the seventh century, possessions of deceased Buddhist monks were auctioned to raise money for temples and monasteries.

In October 2002, eBay acquired PayPal, the e-commerce site that allows anyone with an email address to send and receive online payments.

eBay launched as AuctionWeb on Labor Day of 1995. Founder Pierre Omidyar, then an employee at now-defunct General Magic, also did freelance consulting under the name Echo Bay Technology Group. He wanted to register EchoBay.com, but the name had already been taken by a mining company. So he registered eBay.com instead.

In August 2004, eBay acquired 25 percent of Craigslist, a classified-listings Web site with a devoted following in 120 cities across 25 countries, adding up to over 1 billion page views per month. Craigslist offers a broad array of listings, ranging from personals and job listings to garage sales and apartments for rent.

In April 2005, eBay reported a registered membership of over 147 million users and US net revenues totalling over $404 million for the first quarter of the year.

The legendary Sotheby's auction house was established in 1744. Christie's was founded in 1766. The first upscale American auction house, the American Art Association, was founded in New York in 1883.

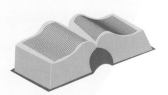

The Oxford English Dictionary first listed the word *auction* in 1595. At that time, auctions were often held in taverns and coffeehouses.

Auction Trivia

The word *auction* derives from the Latin root *auctus*, meaning "a gradual increase."

Winner's curse is when a buyer pays more for an item than it's worth. The buyer wins the auction, but ultimately loses because he or she paid too much.

The rapid-fire talk that professional auctioneers use is called *the chant*. You won't hear any of that on eBay.

Timing is everything: in the 17th century, hourglasses and short candles were used to govern an auction's duration. Bids were accepted until the hourglass emptied or the candle burned out.

There are few areas of commerce that haven't been affected by the auction style of buying and selling. Electricity and radio frequencies are now routinely auctioned, and economics gurus have written volumes about auction theory.

Anatomy of an Auction

An eBay auction is a happy marriage between the physical world and the Internet. The auction process begins when you pull some dusty doodad out of your closet, and it ends when you ship the dusted doodad to its new owner.

But between those two steps, the Internet is where the action is. It's here in cyberspace that your auction reaches the world—where your carefully crafted auction pages inspire bidders to out-do one another, where you watch the bids come in (or not), and in many cases, where you get paid.

Selling on eBay isn't rocket science, but it is more complicated than setting up a card table at a flea market. You need to know how eBay works, how to prepare images and write effective copy, and how to manage the mechanics of the auction.

Most important, you need diligence. We'll stress this point again and again, starting right now: to sell on eBay, you need to pay close attention to every step in the auction process, particularly those that involve customer service. The degree of attention you give your auctions and your customers will directly affect your reputation—and your success—as a seller.

The auction process can seem complex at first, but eBay has set up its system well. If you follow our advice and eBay's rules, you'll do fine. And following the rules begins with knowing what you can and can't sell.

Find the Item

Once you've identified something you want to sell, determine that it's permissible (page 8) and do some research to determine its value (page 18).

Take Photos

Use a digital camera (page 64) or scanner (page 73) to create images that accurately depict the item, including any flaws that may affect its value (page 69), then prepare the images for the Web (page 78).

Create the Auction

Write your copy (page 82), then create the listing page, which includes the title and description (page 38), photos and details (page 40), and payment and shipping information (page 50).

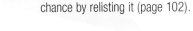

Manage the Auction

While the auction is underway, you can track your progress (page 94), edit listings (page 96), and manage bids (page 98).

No Sale?

Consider giving your item another chance by relisting it (page 102).

Sold!

When the auction ends, contact the winning bidder (page 110), who will pay you, giving you cause to leave positive feedback (page 112).

Pack the Item

Pack the item using materials that will help ensure its safe arrival (page 120). Your packing approach will depend on what you're shipping: large items have unique requirements (page 128).

Ship It!

Determine the most appropriate shipping method (page 48), which may be influenced by whether you're shipping to a domestic or international address. To protect yourself, insure the package (page 55).

Problems?

What can go wrong? Several things, including a buyer who backs out (page 137) or an item breaking during shipping (page 138). A level head, excellent communication skills, and insurance can help when auctions go awry.

Playing by the Rules

What keeps the civilized world from crumbling into anarchy? No, not coffee. Rules. Every community has them, and eBay is no different.

As with civilization itself, much of eBay's success is due to the fact that most people are honest, decent folks. But there will always be bad apples, and rules—and their enforcers—are there to protect us from those nefarious types.

Some of eBay's rules are aimed at simply fostering a pleasant place to do business—where you aren't exposed to foul language, for example. Other rules are designed to protect eBay itself—for example, to keep buyers and sellers from bypassing eBay fees.

And some of eBay's rules have the weight of law behind them. Violating these rules will not only get you in trouble on eBay, it could get you in trouble with the authorities.

When it comes to following the rules on eBay, common sense plays a big role. But some civics lessons never hurt, either. With that in mind, let's look at the laws of the eBay land.

The User Agreement

When you register on eBay, you're presented with a page of eye-numbing text: the User Agreement—nearly 5,000 words of legalese we suspect most people just skip. (We haven't exactly memorized it ourselves.) To complete the registration process, you must accept this agreement.

The User Agreement isn't a scintillating read, but we recommend you at least peruse it. After all, it is a binding contract. To view the User Agreement, click on the Help link at the top of any eBay page. In the Help window that appears, click the Rules & Policies link, then click the Rules & Policies Overview link. The Help window displays links for the User Agreement and more.

Read about eBay's Privacy Policy and learn how to fine-tune your privacy preferences (page 14).

eBay members rate each other by leaving feedback (page 112). Learn about eBay's feedback policies here.

eBay requires complete contact information and has other membership requirements. Learn about them here.

Some rules apply to every eBay member, while other rules are specific to buyers or sellers. We've highlighted some of the most critical rules here, but you can read them all with these links.

You'll laugh! You'll cry! You probably won't read it all. This link displays the User Agreement: the legal contract between you and eBay. Links to the User Agreement and Privacy Policy also appear at the bottom of every eBay page.

The most important eBay policy is Your User Agreement.

eBay Policy categories:

- Privacy: Your privacy is our top priority. Read about is used.
- Feedback: Rules and guidelines about eBay's syste
- Identity: Rules about your contact information and U
- Rules for Everyone: General policies applying to all Trading Policy, and more.
- Rules for Buyers: "Always pay for your purchases".
- Rules for Sellers: Important listing policies and othe off-site sales and the Tax Policy.
- Prohibited and Restricted Items: Can you buy hippo tickets? Find out in our comprehensive list of banne

What *can't* you sell? The list is long, and this link leads to it. See also page 8 for an overview.

Rules for Everyone

Many of eBay's rules apply to buyers as well as sellers. You can find these rules and their links at:

http://pages.ebay.com/help/policies/everyone-ov.html

Of the many rules you'll find at this address, a few deserve particular attention.

Profanity. eBay doesn't tolerate obscenity, and will formally warn and even suspend offenders. So keep it clean when creating a User ID, leaving feedback, posting on discussion boards, or writing copy for a listing. (If a profane word is part of an item's name, use the first letter of the nasty word and then replace the rest of its letters with asterisks. eBay permits this usage when necessary.)

False Contact Information. For auctions to work successfully and smoothly, eBay members need to provide complete and accurate contact information. No nicknames or pseudonyms—remember, the information you're providing is part of the legal agreement between you and eBay. Provide your correct name, address, and phone number when registering.

Spamming. Spam, or unsolicited commercial email, is despised by most computer users, and eBay prohibits members from sending spam to other members. For example, you aren't permitted to add the email addresses of your buyers to a database and then send them your own commercial email solicitations later. At one time, eBay allowed you to use your email address as your eBay User ID, which made it easy for spammers to "harvest" addresses for their dirty deeds. eBay no longer permits you to use your email address as your User ID; now, the only way eBay user email addresses become available to other members is at the end of successful auctions. Use this private information only for appropriate communications related to your auctions.

Rules for Sellers

As a seller, you have additional responsibilities. We strongly recommend you learn about them all by visiting:

http://pages.ebay.com/help/policies/seller-rules-overview.html

Here's a summary of some rules that protect you and your buyers.

Shill Bidding. Shill bidding involves artificially inflating the price of your own auction by bidding on it yourself under another identity or having someone else—a family member, business associate, or friend—do so. This is just plain, old-fashioned cheating. It's also illegal, and there have been cases where the FBI has gotten involved. Shill bidding can get your auction cancelled, your eBay account suspended, or even result in your being referred to a law enforcement agency.

Seller Non-Performance. Once you make a commitment to a sale and the buyer holds up his or her end of the deal, you have a contractual obligation to follow through. You aren't permitted to refuse payment from a buyer at the end of a successful sale. Nor can you fail to deliver an item for which you've accepted payment.

Solicitation of an Off-Site Sale. Now and then, unscrupulous buyers may contact you (via the "Ask seller a question" feature described on page 98) and ask you to circumvent eBay and sell directly to them. This and similar activities are verboten. Rules in this category are aimed at preventing members from avoiding eBay fees while using contact information they've obtained through eBay. For example, if you put a reserve price on one of your auctions (page 21) and the price is not met, it isn't kosher for you to approach any of the low bidders to see if they would like to purchase your item outside of eBay. And remember, if you enter into an agreement with a buyer outside of the eBay realm, you won't be able to avail yourself of any of eBay's fraud-protection features (page 142).

What Can I Sell?

There's a lot of stuff in this world, and not all of it can be sold on eBay. eBay imposes restrictions and even prohibitions in dozens of different categories. Attempt to sell a prohibited item, and eBay may cancel your auction. Try this a few times, and you'll lose your account. Understanding what you can and can't sell can save you headaches later.

Some restrictions reflect obvious legal realities, such as eBay's ban on gun and alcohol sales. Sometimes the legal realities are more complex, especially with intellectual property such as computer software, movies, and music. Software and entertainment companies frequently patrol eBay's auctions, and if you try to sell something that infringes on a copyright or software license agreement, eBay will likely end your auction.

Other eBay restrictions reflect society's wide range of, shall we say, proclivities. eBay walks a fine line when it comes to items intended for "mature audiences"—some of these items are permissible, but many aren't.

eBay has three broad categories of restricted merchandise: prohibited (forget about it), questionable (read the fine print first), and potentially infringing (ditto). What follows are some examples from each category. The full list is much longer, and you'll find it here:

http://pages.ebay.com/help/sell/questions/prohibited-items.html

Prohibited Items

Although many of the following items may be legal to own (and sometimes sell), you can't list them on eBay. But as the following examples show, there are often narrow exceptions to some prohibitions, and eBay's site is the place to learn about them.

Alcohol. Alcohol sales laws are complex and differ from place to place. As a result, eBay prohibits auctions of alcoholic beverages. However, you can sell some unopened, collectible alcohol containers, such as that 1971 can of Partridge Family Malt Liquor you've been saving.

Animals and Wildlife Products.

If you've had it with your chatty myna bird, selling him to the highest bidder is not an option. Some kinds of stuffed birds can be sold, provided your state allows it. There are other exceptions, but generally, eBay doesn't permit the selling of critters and parts of critters.

Firearms. Shotguns, handguns, Civil War guns, BB guns, air guns, flare guns—sell them someplace else. As for ammo, some antique and "demilitarized" ordnance is okay.

Plants and Seeds. If you and your green thumb are interested in plying your plants, first familiarize yourself with the plants and seeds prohibited by the United States Department of Agriculture, as well as the list of state-regulated noxious weeds. You can find links to both on eBay's site.

Tobacco. You can't sell cigarettes, cigars, tobacco, or coupons for these items. However, eBay does make certain allowances for unopened, collectible tobacco packaging. Makes sense—who would want to chew a wad of 1947 Mail Pouch?

Questionable Items

Items in this category can be sold only if they meet certain criteria.

Autographed Items. Forgery is common with sports and movie memorabilia. eBay has extensive guidelines regarding autographs, such as recommending that they be authenticated by an approved authenticator.

Event Tickets. Many states have anti-scalping laws that prohibit the sale of an event ticket for more than its face value. So before you list those tickets for an upcoming playoff game, read the fine print to make sure you're following the rules.

Police Items. Can you sell a police uniform? Yes, if it's obsolete and you say so in your listing. A badge? Probably not, although there are narrow exceptions. A raid jacket with FBI printed on its back? Definitely not.

Used Clothing. Although eBay permits the sale of used clothing, the items must be "thoroughly cleaned according to the manufacturer's instructions." If you're looking to unload those happenin' polyester party shirts, put them through the wash first. Used underwear? Just say no.

Potentially Infringing Items

Software and music piracy is rampant, and it goes without saying that eBay doesn't want any part of it. But the rules regarding intellectual property sales are subtle. Things that may seem legitimate at first glance are often prohibited.

As we mentioned earlier, many software and entertainment companies patrol eBay's listings. A few years ago, eBay established the Verified Rights Owner Program (VeRO) to make it easy for copyright holders to search for and report alleged violations. The VeRO program now has over 5,000 members; many of them have created "About Me" pages that describe their copyright policies, which you can read here:

http://pages.ebay.com/help/community/vero-aboutme.html

If a VeRO member lodges a valid complaint, eBay is obliged to end your listing. Violate this policy repeatedly, and eBay will suspend your account. And note that eBay's privacy policy—which you agree to when you register—permits eBay to share your personal information, including your address and phone number, with VeRO members.

Here are some examples of potentially infringing auctions.

Bundled or OEM Software. You bought a new computer and it came with a copy of Macrosoft Weird. You already have Weird, so you decide to sell the new copy on eBay. Not so fast—most software licenses prohibit the sale of software that came bundled with hardware. (OEM, by the way, stands for original equipment manufacturer.)

Crafts Containing Copyrighted Images. True story: a seller is having success auctioning hand-made, decoupage light switch plates. Suddenly, the auctions are pulled because of an infringement complaint by a VeRO member. The problem: the switch plates contained cartoon characters from a big entertainment company.

Unauthorized Copies. Bootleg recordings of music concerts, videotaped TV shows, pirated copies of video games—don't even think about listing them. And here's a subtle variation: If you sell a personal computer, you can't include software on its hard drive unless you also include the original disks and manuals.

9

Registering on eBay

So you've established that you're not planning to sell anything illegal, immoral, or made of Whooping Crane feathers. If you haven't already joined the eBay community, it's time to do the deed and create an eBay account. (If you're already an eBay member but haven't yet created a seller's account, you might want to skip to page 12.)

Registering on eBay involves supplying some required personal information, reading through and agreeing to eBay's User Agreement and Privacy Policy, and then responding to a confirmation email that eBay will send you. The entire process should take only a few minutes.

To begin, go to eBay's home page (www.ebay.com, as if you need us to tell you that). Next, click the Register link at the very top of the page.

And if you've already been browsing on eBay, you don't even need to go to the home page to register—you'll find a Register link at the top of each page. (After you register and sign in, this link disappears.)

Each of these links will take you to the same place: the Enter Information page, where the joys of registration begin.

Step 1. Enter Information

On the Enter Information page (right), supply your contact information and agree to the eBay User Agreement and Privacy Policy.

Step 2. Choose User ID and Password

Your eBay User ID is your moniker, your handle, your badge of honor for all your eBay endeavors. For tips on creating a User ID, see the sidebar on the opposite page.

Think up a password and type it twice. Avoid the obvious, such as your spouse's birth date, your phone number, or your pet's name. (The security-o-meter shows how secure eBay considers your password to be.) Choose a password that's memorable to you and tricky enough to stop those with evil hearts. Consider combining letters and numbers—for example, *100nyb1n* instead of *loonybin*. **Tip:** Never give your password to anyone.

eBay will suggest a few possible User IDs based on the information you entered on the previous screen, or you can create your own.

Choose a secret question, then type the answer. This allows you to create a new password should you forget your current one.

Happy with your choices? Click Continue.

Step 3. Confirm Your Email

eBay sends a confirmation email to the address you provided. Its subject is *Complete Your eBay Registration*. Didn't get the email? Make sure it wasn't deleted or stashed somewhere by your email program's junk mail filter.

Inside this email is a button that links back to eBay's site. To confirm and complete the registration, click the button. In a few moments, your browser will display eBay's congratulations.

First name

Last name

Street address

City

State / Province
--Select--

Zip / Postal code

Country
United States

Primary telephone
(   )   -   ext.:

Secondary telephone (Optional)
(   )   -   ext.:

Date of Birth
--Month--   --Day--   Year

Important: A valid email address is required to complete registration.

Email address

Examples: myname@yahoo.com, myname@example.com, etc.

Re-enter email address

eBay User Agreement and Privacy Policy (Printer-friendly version)

eBay User Agreement and Privacy Policy
User Agreement

THE FOLLOWING DESCRIBES THE TERMS ON WHICH EBAY OFFERS YOU ACCESS TO OUR
SERVICES.

Welcome to the user agreement (the "Agreement" or "User Agreement") for
eBay Inc. If you reside outside of the United States, the party you are

Please check the box below:
☐ I agree to the following:
  • I accept the User Agreement and Privacy Policy above.
  • I may receive communications from eBay and I understand that I can change my notification
    preferences at any time in My eBay.

Continue >

eBay has strict policies regarding false contact information (see page 7), so tell the whole truth and nothing but.

Specify your date of birth.

Enter your email address twice. eBay will send a confirmation email to that address. **Note:** eBay may also require you to enter a valid debit or credit card number, especially if you have a free email account through Hotmail, Yahoo, or a similar provider. This is simply to verify your identity; your card isn't charged.

Read through the User Agreement and Privacy Policy. You can also print these items for some thrilling bathtub reading.

Confirm that you accept the User Agreement and Privacy Policy and acknowledge that eBay will send you email now and then. You can choose from many different ways to receive communications from eBay, if you choose to receive them at all (see page 15).

Proofread the page one last time, then click Continue.

Tips for Choosing (and Changing) Your User ID

Choose a User ID you like—it will be your name on eBay, and the way fellow eBayers will come to recognize you. If you'll be specializing in a particular type of item, consider an ID that reflects your wares, such as MustardMaven.

Your User ID must be at least two characters long and can contain a combination of letters, numerals, and certain symbols. Your User ID cannot be an email address or URL.

A User ID cannot contain profanity, nor can it contain spaces, tab characters, or any of the following symbols: @, &, ', <, or >. Also prohibited: consecutive underscores (__), and the word eBay (that's reserved for eBay employees). And you can't begin your User ID with the letter "e" followed by numbers, an underscore (_), or a dash (-).

You can change your User ID, and you may want to if you change the types of items you sell. But you can alter your ID only once in a 30-day period. When you have your new ID, your old feedback will follow you, but a "changed ID" icon will appear alongside your new ID for 30 days.

Creating a Seller's Account

You've joined the club and are now a registered eBay member. Perhaps you've done a bit of buying to gather some feedback (page 23), and now you're ready to start selling. Before you start, create a seller's account.

If you're already registered on eBay, why do you need to create a separate account for selling? One reason is security. To keep out the riffraff, eBay requires an additional level of information about its sellers.

Another reason is that selling on eBay also involves paying eBay—for the listing fees charged when you begin an auction, and for the commission fees charged when an auction ends. Part of creating a seller's account is telling eBay how you plan to pony up.

To create a seller's account, you must make your way through several screens, entering information and making choices along the way. Have a credit or debit card and your checkbook close by before you start.

Don't have either? Or don't want to use them? It is possible to sell on eBay without providing this information. If you go through the ID Verify process described on the opposite page, you can pay your seller's fees by check or money order. We don't recommend this, though. eBay imposes a $25 outstanding balance limit on seller's accounts, freezing accounts when they exceed that amount. And because mailed payments can take a week or more to be credited, you'll need to keep the checks flowing to keep your auctions going.

Step 1. Click the Sell Button

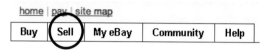

This button sits in the main navigation bar at the top of every eBay page. After you click Sell, the Sell page appears. Click the Sell Your Item button on that page. If you're already signed in, you'll go directly to the Create a Seller's Account page. If you aren't signed in, a sign-in screen appears; type your User ID and password, then click the Sign-In Securely button.

Step 2. Click the Create Seller's Account button

Step 3. Provide Identification

For eBay to verify your identity, you must provide a credit or debit card number and place a checking account on file. (As noted on the following page, you can use ID Verify instead of providing this information.) eBay won't charge these accounts unless you authorize the transaction. There are two screens to work through: one for the plastic card and one for the checking account. When providing your debit/credit card information, double check and be sure that the cardholder information that appears is the same as your billing address. If there is a discrepancy, be sure to edit the address. This will prevent confusion down the line.

Tip: It can take a half a minute or so for eBay to verify a checking account.

Step 4. Specify How to Pay Seller Fees

It takes money to make money. Fees are charged for listing and selling items (see page 16), and you need to specify how you plan to pay. Choose the checking account or card you provided in the previous step. If you change your mind later, you can use My eBay (page 14) to change your payment method.

Create Seller's Account: Select How to Pay Selling Fees

1. Enter Credit or Debit Card   2. Enter Checking Account   ③ Select How to Pay S

Please select how you want to pay selling fees. Fees are only charged when you list o owe fees, they are automatically charged each month. You can always check your bal you pay selling fees in My eBay.

How you would like to pay selling fees?

◉ **Checking account**
Bank: Bank
Routing number:

Checking account
number: XXXX8697

○ **Credit or debit card**
Card type:
Card number: XXXX
XXXX XXXX
Expiration date: 10 / 2005

Step 5. Sell!

If all has gone well, your seller's account is active and you're ready to rumble. If you'd like to create a listing now, see page 36.

When you check your email, you'll find one from eBay congratulating you on becoming a seller. You'll receive notification emails from eBay when activities take place with your card, such as updating the credit card information on another account that uses the same card.

Background Check: The ID Verify Option

When a soap opera heartthrob returns from the dead with a completely new face, the only way he can prove his identity is by telling information only he would know.

ID Verify works similarly. A service of eBay and VeriSign (a big Internet security company), ID Verify asks you personal financial questions that only you can answer accurately.

You might use ID Verify if you'd prefer to keep your credit or debit card and checking account information private, or if you don't have one or both of these things.

Becoming ID-verified has another benefit: it enables you to create Buy it Now auctions (page 21) even if you don't have the 10 feedback ratings normally required to do so. And some sellers simply believe this additional stamp of approval makes their auctions more tempting to potential bidders.

To begin the ID Verify process, click the Site Map link at the top of almost any eBay page, then click the ID Verify link under Marketplace Safety.

Tip: The site map is a great way to quickly get around on eBay's vast site.

You'll begin the verification by entering your address, phone number, date of birth, and Social Security and driver's license numbers. All of this information will be submitted to VeriSign, but not stored or even viewed by eBay.

After VeriSign confirms this first round of information, you'll need to enter even more, such as the amount of your car payment, the digits of a particular credit card, or a previous street address. The theory here is that only you can accurately answer these questions, so you must be who you say you are.

If you pass muster, you'll receive a verification email from VeriSign, and eBay will add a special icon (❧) to your feedback profile. This icon will appear for 12 months, after which time you can renew if you like.

At this writing, ID verification costs $5. Is it worth it? Yes, if don't want eBay verifying your banking information or don't want to give out your credit or debit card information. As for building the trust of potential bidders, we think your feedback tells a far better story than a nod from VeriSign.

My eBay for Sellers: The Big Picture

If you've been buying on eBay, you may already be familiar with My eBay—it's your mission control for all of your eBay activities. With My eBay, you can manage your eBay account, keep track of your buying and selling, view and leave feedback, and specify your preferences for how eBay works for you.

You can buy and sell without using My eBay, but you'll work a lot harder than you have to. Even if you buy and sell only occasionally, you can benefit from My eBay.

We'll be looking at various aspects of My eBay throughout this book. Now, we want to focus on one aspect of My eBay: its Preferences screens, where you can make changes to your contact, billing, and user information; specify how eBay keeps in touch with you; update your payment preferences; specify features within My eBay itself; and much more.

If you're new to eBay selling, some of the options we're about to describe may seem confusing. Don't feel like you must absorb everything here before continuing; indeed, you can skip this section and return to it later, after you have created an auction or two and are ready to put My eBay to work.

Setting My eBay Preferences

To specify My eBay preferences, use My eBay's Preferences pages.

Step 1. Go to My eBay.

To access My eBay, click the My eBay button in the navigation bar that appears near the top of nearly every eBay page. If you haven't yet signed in, you may have to do so after clicking the My eBay button.

Step 2. Click the Preferences link.

You'll find the Preferences link under My Account in the My eBay Views area, which runs along the left side of the window. This area is mission control for My eBay.

Two Useful General Preferences

The General Preferences area of the Preferences page has two options that you might want to tweak. To access these options, scroll down to General Preferences and, in the Other General Preferences area, click the Show link.

Staying signed in. You have the option to remain signed in to your eBay account unless you specifically sign out. If you're the only person who uses your computer, you probably want to avoid typing your User ID and password over and over again. But bear in mind that remaining signed in will make it possible for anyone who sits at your computer to access your bidding and buying pages.

You'll want to avoid this option if you're working at a shared computer—in a coffee shop, for example.

Viewing email addresses. It's often useful to see bidders' email addresses along with their User IDs after the close of your auctions (see page 98). Specify that preference here.

Other general preferences		Hide
Keep me signed in on this computer	☐ Yes	
	Apply	
Show User IDs with email addresses	☑ Yes	
	Email addresses will be displayed for 14 days after a transaction ends.	
	Apply	

More Preference Settings

Here's an overview of some of the other account and seller preferences you might want to adjust. To display the options for a given category, click its Show link.

The options in this area let you specify some important selling-related preferences. Some of the choices you make here affect the default choices made for you when you create a listing; others let you choose options that help promote your auctions.

eBay wants to keep in touch with you, and this link leads to a page that lets you control that communication. Many notification options deal with buying, but some pertain to selling. To receive a confirmation email when you begin a new auction, check the *Listing confirmation emails* box. To receive a daily status email detailing auctions in which you're bidding or selling, check the *Daily status emails* box (see page 94).

To display the options for a particular preference, click its Show link.

Change your PayPal preferences, edit your payment address, or choose to use eBay's Checkout feature (see page 53).

Do you sell a lot? You can offer a variety of payment and shipping deals, such as allowing buyers to make one payment when they purchase multiple items from you within 30 days.

Spread the word: these options let you control how your listings are promoted. We find the default options work fine.

You can customize the invoices and end-of-auction emails that eBay sends to your buyers, but we recommend a more personal approach (see page 111).

You can choose to block certain buyers from all your auctions here. For the pros and cons of blocking bidders, see page 100.

Preferences   Show all

Use Preferences to change your eBay settings for email, payment, selling, etc.

Notification Preferences

Receive emails and other communications from eBay.   Edit

Selling Preferences

Sell Your Item form and listings   Show
Edit your Sell Your Item form preferences and other listing preferences.

Payment from buyers   Show
Edit Checkout, PayPal, and other payment options you offer buyers.

Shipping and discounts   Show
Offer shipping discounts on combined purchases, UPS shipping rate options, etc.

Promoting Similar Items on eBay Pages and Emails   Show
Promote your items in emails and on item pages.

Logos and branding   Show
Display your logo and send customized emails to buyers.

Buyer requirements   Show
Block certain eBay users from buying your items.

General Preferences

Searching and buying   Show
Display your recently viewed items and searches while you shop.

My eBay   Hide

Display this My eBay view first   [My Summary ▾]

Show time in My eBay in this format   ⦿ Time left (5d 02h 26m)
                                         ○ End time/date (Feb-10 07:42:42)

Display Help content in My eBay   ☑ Yes

Show Personalized Picks   ☑ Yes

                                         [Apply]

Retrieve items removed from My eBay   [Retrieve Removed Items]

Do you spend more time selling than buying? If so, choose *All Selling* from the drop-down menu. Thereafter, clicking the My eBay button takes you to the All Selling page instead of the Summary page.

Did you remove an auction from My eBay by mistake (see page 95)? This button will restore it.

Seller's Fees: You've Got to Pay to Play

Seller's fees are the cost of doing business on eBay. eBay gives you a worldwide venue for selling (almost) anything you like—in return, you pay a small *insertion fee* when an auction begins.

One of many reasons eBay handles over 30 million auctions a month is that its fees tend to be reasonable. It can cost as little as 25 cents to make a product available to the millions of people who visit eBay's site each month.

To help your listings stand apart, eBay offers extra-cost *listing upgrades* that range in price from a dime to $39.95. Some of these options are great investments that can pay for themselves in higher bids. Others are gimmicky—they may be a herd of cash cows for eBay, but they're unlikely to improve your sales all that much.

Insertion fees are only part of eBay's cut. The rest comes when an auction ends with a winning bidder, at which time you pay a *final value fee*, a kind of commission whose amount is a percentage of whatever your auction fetched.

We'll explore many of eBay's listing options and upgrades in detail later. To give you a feel for what your auctions will cost, here's an overview of eBay's fees and listing services. For the latest pricing updates, go to:

http://pages.ebay.com/help/sell/fees.html

Insertion Fees

eBay charges a non-refundable fee for listing an item. This fee is based on the item's starting price (its minimum bid). For reserve price auctions (which we cover on page 21), the fee is based on the reserve price.

Starting or Reserve Price	Insertion Fee
$0.01–$0.99	$0.25
$1.00–$9.99	$0.35
$10.00–$24.99	$0.60
$25.00–$49.99	$1.20
$50.00–$199.99	$2.40
$200.00–$499.99	$3.60
$500.00 and above	$4.80

Tip: There's an exception to every rule. If your item doesn't sell and you re-list within 90 days and the second auction is successful, eBay will refund your insertion fee for the second listing. For more details, see page 102.

Fees for Reserve Price Auctions

The insertion fee for a reserve price auction is based on the "secret" price you've specified as the lowest you're willing to take for your item. For example, if the reserve price is $75, the insertion fee is $2.40.

You'll also pay extra for the privilege of creating a reserve price auction, although eBay will refund this additional fee if your item sells.

Reserve Price	Additional Fee
$0.01-$49.99	$1.00
$50.00-$199.99	$2.00
$200.00 and up	1% of reserve price (maximum fee of $100)

Final Value Fees: eBay's Cut

When a successful auction ends, eBay charges a fee based on the final sale price or high bid. For reserve-price auctions, the final value fee is charged only if your minimum bid was met.

Closing High Bid	Final Value Fee
$25 or less	5.25% of auction's closing price
$25.01–$1,000	5.25% of the initial $25 ($1.31) plus 2.75% of the remaining closing balance
Over $1,000	5.25% of the initial $25 ($1.31) plus 2.75% of the initial $25–$1,000 ($26.81), plus 1.50% of the remaining closing balance

For example, if your limited-edition Pee Wee Herman action figure sells for $328, eBay's cut is $9.64. If your Monkees drum set commands $1125, eBay gets $30.

How Low Should You Go?

So why wouldn't you just start every auction at the low, low price of 99 cents—with no reserve—in order to minimize the insertion fee?

You certainly can, although if bidding is slow for some reason, you risk having to sell your item for less than its value. (Remember, if you don't set a reserve price, you're obligated to sell at whatever price the winning bid is.) And even if bidding does go nice and high, you'll still pay eBay more later, when it comes time to pay the final value fee.

Pony Up: Paying Your Seller's Fees

When you created your seller's account, eBay assigned you to a billing cycle. Depending on when you created your seller's account, your billing date will either be the middle of the month or the last day of the month. On this date, eBay will total up your fees from the previous month and email you an invoice within about five days.

To learn your billing date and get your current account balance, go to the eBay site map (its link is near the top of nearly every eBay page) and then click the link named View Your Account Status or Invoice.

You can pay your seller's fees in any of four ways.

PayPal. You can have the amount of your current invoice charged to your PayPal account. You can also set up an automatic monthly payment.

Credit Card. You can keep a credit card on file with eBay to pay your seller's fees automatically. Your credit card will be charged a week or so after you receive your seller's fee invoice.

eBay Direct Pay. Give eBay your checking account and routing numbers, and your checking account will be debited by the amount of your current invoice. As with PayPal, you can also set up automatic monthly payments.

Checks and money orders. If you can't or don't want to keep your personal financial information on file with eBay, you can choose to pay in this manner. eBay takes a week or more to process checks or money orders, and that doesn't include holidays and weekends. You must include a payment coupon, available at http://cgi3.ebay.com/aw-cgi/eBayISAPI.dll?PayCoupon.

Is the Price Right? Pricing Your Auctions

You've created your seller's account and familiarized yourself with eBay's rules and fees. You're ready for action—and auctions.

But what is that dusty doodad worth? What should be the auction's starting price? And how much can you expect to get when the bidding dust settles?

To find out what something is worth, do your homework. eBay itself is the best place to start—by searching completed auctions, you can see what similar items have sold for recently. The category-specific areas of eBay's discussion boards are another excellent resource.

And for many categories of collectibles, such as coins and sports memorabilia, authentication and grading services will give your item the benefit of a professional's eye and seal of approval.

Bottom line: Before you begin the process of listing an item, spend some quality time figuring out what the thing is worth.

Do-it-Yourself Appraisals: A Checklist

Here's a list of steps you might want to perform to assess an item's value.

Search completed auctions. The best way to gauge how much your item may fetch is to see what similar items have sold for recently (see opposite page for details).

Read the literature. For many types of collectibles, there are printed price handbooks, collector's guides, specialty magazines, and Web sites that can help you valuate an item. Know your subject.

Surf the boards. eBay's discussion boards have category-specific forums where eBayers of all experience levels ask and answer questions covering eBay's most popular categories (see page 25).

Consider an authentication and grading service. The more collectible your item, the more you may benefit from an expert's opinion. Some companies will evaluate the condition and authenticity of coins, stamps, comics, sports memorabilia, and even Beanie Babies. Include their evaluation information in your auction, and you stand a far better chance of earning top dollar.

For serious collectors, phrases such as "very good condition" mean very specific things. A grading service will examine your item and report on its condition using the industry-standard lingo that collectors look for (see Appendix B for more details). Many grading services will also seal your item in special packaging, complete with a serial number or barcode that corresponds to an entry in the service's registry.

eBay has assembled a list of grading and authentication services at www.ebay.com/help/community/auth-overview.html. You'll pay for these expert opinions, of course. If you think you have a genuinely valuable item, it pays to be an informed seller.

Tip: Putting a new shine on that old silver dollar or other antique will decrease its value in the eyes of a collector. If you aren't an expert on a particular item and you think its age and condition may be among its defining features, find out more before you clean it, refinish it, or otherwise prepare it for sale.

Searching Completed Auctions

The best way to predict the future is to study the past. Checking out completed listings is a great way to estimate what your item might sell for, what a reasonable starting price might be, and how many similar items have been sold recently. (And we mean *recently:* unfortunately, eBay reports on only auctions that ended within the previous two weeks.)

You can customize search options—for example, to show only those items whose prices are listed in US dollars.

In this example, we're searching for the coveted Dukes of Hazzard action figures we hope to list soon.
Tip: Try doing multiple searches with different spellings. For example, after searching for *dukes of hazzard*, search for *dukes of hazard*.

To search completed auctions only, check this box.

To sort the list of search results by price or ending date, click the column headings.

Find items that resemble yours? Examine their auctions to see how closely they match. Is your item in better or worse condition? Does it include more or fewer accessories? What were the other items' starting prices? By answering questions like these, you can get a feel for what your starting price should be and how much you might expect to get.

If you find an item that's very similar to yours and decide that you're ready to create your new listing, click this link to get a head start: eBay will copy that auction's category (and, with some items, its description, too) to your new listing.

Note: When you do a completed-listings search, eBay requires that you sign in. If you haven't registered yet, the time is now.

Step 1. Click the Advanced Search link in the navigation bar that appears at the top of every eBay page.

Step 2. Specify your search criteria and click the Search button. If eBay's sign-in screen appears, sign in.

Several bids can indicate high demand.

Tips: Bookmark the Advanced Search page for fast access. And if you've done a search for current auctions and you'd like to apply the search to completed auctions, click the Completed Items box in the Search Options area located at the left edge of the browser window, then click the Show Items button below the search options.

Pricing Strategies

As we'll see in the next chapter, when you create an auction, you can set a *starting* price, a *reserve* price, and a *Buy It Now* price. The only price you *must* specify is the starting price, but there are times when you might want to employ a reserve price, take advantage of the Buy It Now option, or both.

It's a game of strategy. By pricing smart, you can increase bidders' interest in your item and increase your bottom line, too. Here's a look at each option and how they relate to one another.

Pricing Scenarios: Some Examples

You can combine starting, reserve, and Buy It Now pricing in an uncountable number of ways. Here are several pricing scenarios and our take on them.

Where to Begin? Setting a Starting Price

On page 18, we discussed ways to determine your item's potential value. It's important to have an idea of how much an item might fetch, but potential value and starting price are two different beasts. You may think your *Raymond Burr Sings Rolling Stones* album is worth $45, but you wouldn't want to start the bidding at that amount. You want a starting price that stirs up excitement among potential bidders and convinces them they might just score a real deal.

So what should that price be? In a word, low. Or at least low enough to get bidders' attention. Look at completed auctions that are similar to yours (page 19), see where they started, and come up with an enticing price. If you're worried about losing your shirt due to unusually slow bidding or hot competition, consider stringing up a safety net: a reserve price.

Tip: Price Right to Save Insertion Fees

What's the difference between $24.99 and $25.01? 60 cents. At this writing, that's the difference in eBay's insertion fees between those two starting prices. To save on insertion fees, consider setting your starting price at a point just below where the next insertion fee tier kicks in. Use the table on page 16 as your guide.

Pricing	Comments
Starting: $1 **Reserve:** $0 **Buy It Now:** $0	You're either unconcerned that your item will be undervalued (maybe it isn't worth much to begin with) or you're convinced it's so hot that bidders will drive the price up. This pricing gets bidders' attention and keeps insertion fees low.
Starting: $9.99 **Reserve:** $95 **Buy It Now:** $99.99	If you're going to protect yourself with a reserve price, consider a lower starting price to entice bidders. Sometimes a reserve price can discourage bidding.
Starting: $24.99 **Reserve:** $0 **Buy It Now:** $49.99	Here's a reasonable starting price, with a Buy it Now price for the impatient. The lack of a reserve price may help jump-start bidding.
Starting: $129 **Reserve:** $0 **Buy It Now:** $0	Danger, Will Robinson! Unless this is a pricey or big-ticket item, the high starting price may discourage bidders. Better to start lower and, if you must, specify a reserve price, too.

Creating a Reserve Auction

Sure, you can get bidders' attention by setting a starting price of $2.99 for your Limoges gold-leafed clock. But if bad luck strikes and you don't get the bidding you anticipated, you could end up selling your treasure for much less than it's worth.

By setting a reserve price, you can protect yourself against nightmares like this. In a reserve auction, you specify a "secret" price that represents the minimum you're willing to accept for your item. If that amount is not met, your auction ends without a winning bidder.

This practice may sound great but the fact is, reserve auctions are a turn-off to many bidders. Some bidders skip them entirely. They may not want to play the guessing game necessary to find your secret price—it can get annoying to place bid after bid, only to see "Reserve not yet met" each time you do. And the fact that you've specified a reserve is a strong hint that there isn't a dynamite bargain to be found in your listing.

Rather than setting a reserve price, we think you're better off doing the research necessary to see what your competition is up to, setting a starting price you find reasonable, and putting together a great title and description, with excellent photos.

If you feel you must go the reserve-auction route, specify a reserve price that is the minimum amount you're willing to accept for your item, then set a low, low starting price. Consider mentioning your reserve price in the item description.

As noted on page 16, specifying a reserve price will cost you slightly more in listing fees. If your item sells, however, eBay will refund this extra charge.

Instant Gratification: Buy It Now

The Buy It Now option is for buyers and sellers who crave instant gratification. When you specify a Buy It Now price, a bidder can buy your item at that price and end the auction immediately.

For buyers, the advantage of a Buy It Now auction is immediacy. There's no need to wait until an auction closes, no need to check email for outbid notices, and no worries about losing an item to another bidder. Buy It Now turns your auction into a classified ad.

Always make the starting price lower than the Buy It Now price.

Yes, it's the age-old retail-pricing trick—because $14.99 sounds cheaper than $15.

As with any other auction, shoppers can place a conventional bid by clicking Place Bid.

If the shopper has to have it now, he or she can click Buy It Now.

If someone wants your item now, they pay your price and the deal is done.

On eBay's search-results pages, an auction that has a Buy It Now price is indicated by a special badge. The categories listings and search-results pages also have a Buy It Now tab that shoppers can click to view only Buy It Now auctions. And by using the advanced search page, shoppers can restrict searches to only those auctions that have a Buy It Now option.

No bids yet—as soon as one comes in, the Buy It Now option disappears and the auction continues.

The Buy It Now badge also appears on the listing page itself.

The Buy It Now option obviously has appeal for sellers, too. If you're listing something that's time-sensitive—for example, concert tickets—you may be able to get top dollar right away. If you know how much you want to get and don't want to play the auction waiting game, Buy It Now may be for you. Just be sure to look over completed auctions of similar items and don't set your price below what the items are typically selling for. And remember that you'll pay between 5 and 25 cents more in listing fees, depending on the sale price, to specify the Buy It Now option.

Goodwill Hunting:
Advice on Seller's Etiquette

The phenomenon of eBay is just that: phenomenal. When you go to a brick-and-mortar store, you can touch things, try them on, and decide if that chair is just the right shade of blue for the sunroom. Even when you shop from a mail-order catalog, you can always dial a customer service number and contact a real company in case of questions or problems. And the products in the catalogs are clearly described and are photographed by professionals.

Not so on eBay. Here, you are the advertising agency, product photographer, customer service department, accounts receivable staff, and shipping department. With eBay, people buy products sight unseen, send money into the abyss, and receive their packages on the front porch. Yes, eBay has a system of checks and balances to keep things running smoothly, safely, and fairly. But it's still up to each seller and buyer to make eBay hum.

An eBay bidder is making a leap of faith in doing business with you, particularly if you're a new seller. Acknowledge that faith by treating your customers with the greatest respect. They trust you—now earn it.

We'll be elaborating on the rules of seller etiquette throughout this book. Here's a summary of the key rules by which every good eBay seller lives.

Give Them Facts

Gather as much information as you can about each item you're selling: its age, manufacturer, weight, and so on. If it has a chip, crack, dent, scratch, imperfection, discoloration, or makes a funny sound when you squeeze it, say so. The more "collectible" an item, the more details bidders will want. One key to a successful auction: no surprises.

Simplify Their Lives

Make life easy for bidders by listing—in plain sight—your shipping, handling, payment, insurance, return policy, and other requirements. Again, your goal is to avoid surprises.

Keep it Reasonable

You're permitted to charge a reasonable amount for packaging, shipping, and handling. The key word here is *reasonable*. Charging $25 to ship a Pez dispenser won't cut it. Make your shipping charges realistic, and never, ever mark up insurance costs.

Keep in Touch

Nothing makes a buyer feel better than knowing that your goal is to make this transaction quick and painless. Respond to questions quickly, courteously, and in detail. Keep the buyer informed.

Be Polite

Indeed, bend over backwards being polite. Don't get angry; try to find a way to resolve issues. Take a deep breath before responding to an angry email.

Insure Your Shipments

Whether you ship postcards or pianos, insuring your shipments is just good business. We require buyers to purchase insurance for virtually every auction, whether we choose to self-insure or we avail ourselves of the insurance provided by our shipper (see page 55).

If It's Broken, Fix It

Give your buyers a money-back guarantee, no matter the reason. If they simply don't like what they bought, you can ask them to pay return shipping, but do refund their money. Customers aren't always right—but it's good business to pretend that they are. Note that we do make an exception in one area. When selling software or other media that can be easily copied, you should note in your auction that the item can be returned only if the box is unopened or if, upon examination, the media is clearly damaged or defective. You don't want mischievous buyers copying software and returning it for a refund.

Feedback Rules

Never underestimate the power of positive feedback, both given and received. When buyers pay promptly, leave them positive feedback right away. It's how everyone establishes good standing as an eBay member. Give good feedback, and you're likely to get it, too—assuming you've earned it.

Provide Buyer Protection

eBay recommends a variety of authentication and escrow services that provide buyers with an extra measure of protection and assurance. You may want to use these options, particularly if you're a new seller or you're selling items that are very valuable. Using these services tells bidders that you're looking to do business fairly and professionally (see page 18).

Advice for New eBayers: Go Shopping

Getting your foot in the seller's door means showing potential buyers that you can be trusted. On eBay, reputation takes the form of feedback (see page 112). eBay members view this feedback by clicking the numeral that appears within parenthesis alongside another member's User ID.

mygruffin (0) 🔒

To view another member's feedback, click the numeral.

Every good eBayer's goal is to acquire positive feedback. But it often takes feedback to get feedback. Getting started as a seller can be difficult with that ominous goose egg looming

next to your User ID. To highlight your newbie status even more, a shiny New ID icon appears if you've been a member for 30 or fewer days. Without feedback to examine, potential bidders may hesitate to bid.

Our suggestion: do some buying. If you're new to eBay and haven't done any wheeling and

dealing yet, start racking up positive feedback by being a stellar buyer. eBay's Feedback Forum indicates whether each item of feedback evaluates you as a buyer or as a seller. If potential bidders see that you've rated well as a buyer, they can at least be reassured that you know how business is done on eBay.

Ask Around: The eBay Community

As you use eBay, you're bound to have questions. Some questions might be technical: How do I add some fancy formatting to my listing? What software should I use to improve my pictures?

Other questions might be logistical: How do I deal with a problem bidder? Still others might be strategic: What are the hot categories these days?

We've addressed the most common questions in this book, but a lot more information is available within eBay's vast site. eBay's online help is one place to look, but the best advice often comes from your fellow eBay members, people who have faced and solved the same problem that kept you awake last night.

eBay's community area is an online metropolis filled with newsletters, event calendars, and bustling discussion areas where eBay members and staff exchange messages by the millions. eBay has always worked to cultivate the image of a friendly community, and these forums are a cornerstone of that effort.

In fact, some critics complain that eBay relies too heavily on its members helping one another. Maybe, maybe not. eBay staffers do hang out in the eBay community and are often genuinely helpful. But in the end, it's other members who have made eBay's forums and online workshops great places to learn, share, gossip, and fritter away entire afternoons.

Won't You Be My Neighbor?

To step into the eBay community, click the Community button at the top of nearly every eBay page. **Tip:** You can quickly jump to specific community areas by using eBay's site map link, which also appears at the top of every eBay page.

Everyone's a critic. Your reputation is based on the feedback you leave and receive. Use the Feedback Forum to leave and read feedback and more (see page 112).

Get the 411. Enter a User ID to access a member's profile, items for sale, and more. eBay displays exact and close matches. You can also search by email address, although you must sign in and won't get as much information.

Enter the fray. A cornucopia of conversation, advice, and idle chitchat, this is where eBayers go to ask and learn and see and be seen. Learn more on the opposite page.

Join up. Find groups of eBayers with similar interests. The eBay Sellers area contains groups whose members share tips, and critique each other's listings. You can also start your own group, if you'd like.

Where to Turn?

You're stumped, curious, or bored—or maybe all three. Should you turn to a discussion board, a chat room, or the Answer Center?

Chat rooms. The chat rooms are swell if you want to while away the hours, but they aren't always useful information sources. Each chat area is an ongoing conversation: one eBayer types a question or comment, another replies, and the conversation goes on. There are category-specific chat rooms, but the conversations tend to stray quickly.

Tip: If you're having trouble getting in touch with a buyer or seller, the Emergency Contact chat room is a good place to get help, though the conversation can veer off-topic here, too. When posting to this chat room and anywhere else on eBay, never divulge someone's personal information—use only a buyer's User ID.

As for the remaining two information sources, they overlap in many ways, but each has some unique advantages.

The Answer Center. The Answer Center is more succinct and focused—just a couple dozen topics, each dealing with eBay itself or with related technical issues.

On the downside, questions come into the Answer Center so quickly that they tend to disappear below the bottom of the page within a day or two, or even within a few hours.

Tip: If there's an Answer Center question you're particularly interested in, you can *watch* it—monitor the question and be notified by email when someone posts an answer. It beats checking back all the time to see if someone has replied.

To watch a question, click the Sign In link near the top of the page. Supply your User ID and password, then click the link for the question you want to watch. A Watch This Question link appears above the question box. Click this link to specify your watch options (below).

Discussion boards. The discussion boards are more free-wheeling than the Answer Center. While many of the discussion boards cover the same topics as the Answer Center, there are also boards that don't relate to eBay itself, but to everything that people buy and sell using eBay—computers, collectibles, and so on.

Each board has a list of topics called *discussions,* and each discussion has a series of postings called *threads*. You can explore a board's discussions by simply browsing through them, or you can search for specific words or for postings from specific users. Just click the Search button at the top of a board page.

Tip: The Seller Central board is aimed at you. It's a great place to look for advice on everything from dealing with troublesome buyers to becoming a full-time seller.

Another tip: eBay's online workshops are live events, but if you miss them, you aren't out of luck—they're archived in the Workshops discussion board.

Community Rules

As with other areas of eBay, the community has its rules and regulations. Violating these rules can have a variety of consequences.

If you're having a problem or think another member has committed a violation, take it up with eBay. You'll find all the rules at eBay's Board Usage Policy page:

http://pages.ebay.com/help/policies/everyone-boards.html

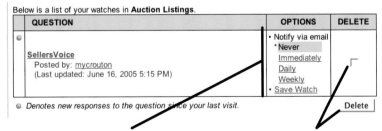

To be notified when answers come in, click Immediately (you'll get an email each time someone answers), Daily (you'll get one email a day), or Weekly (once a week).

To stop watching a question, check this box, then click the Delete button. You can also stop by clicking the Stop Watching Question link that appears above the question box.

More Ways to Stay In the Know

You've gotten a feel for eBay's rules and regulations, you've set up a seller's account, and maybe you've explored the community areas of eBay's site. You're just about ready to start selling.

Before we move into the process of actually creating an auction listing, let's end our tour of eBay basics with a few more tips and resources for getting acquainted and staying current with eBay. Learning the ropes is crucial, but staying up to speed with eBay's ever-evolving site and rules is just as important.

We'll also look at eBay's Help Center. It's the place to go to get answers to your selling and buying questions.

And finally, we'd be remiss if we didn't mention this book's companion Web site, located at www.ebaymatters.com. We post frequent book updates, tips for sellers, tidbits about new eBay features, and eBay in the news. If you use a newsreader (such as NewsGator for Windows or NetNewsWire for the Mac), you can subscribe to our full-text feed and get each posting delivered directly to your newsreader.

(If you aren't familiar with newsreaders, do a Google search for *introduction to RSS*, then go exploring.)

Another Spin Around the Community

On previous pages, we introduced the Community area and its message boards and chat rooms. There's more to the Community area, and here's a look at some of it. To see the Community area for yourself, click the Community button at the top of most pages.

News. The News section will help keep you informed about feature enhancements, system outages and fixes, promotions, and events. You'll also find a link to *The Chatter,* eBay's monthly newsletter on all aspects of buying and selling.

If you use newsreader software, you can have eBay's general and system announcements delivered directly to you. To subscribe to general announcements, enter the following URL in your newsreader: http://www2.ebay.com/aw/marketing.xml. For system announcements, subscribe to http://www2.ebay.com/aw/announce.xml.

Education. With the links in the Education area of the Community home page, you can attend online workshops, join a mentoring group, and develop your skills with audio and video tours.

Resources from Around the Web

eBay isn't the only source of auction news and wisdom. Here are some that we rely on—and one that we create ourselves.

Sell It on eBay: The Web Site. As we mentioned at left, this book has a companion Web site, which should be a daily part of your eBay diet. Head to www.ebaymatters.com for news, updates, and commentary on all manner of eBay matters.

AuctionBytes. This site (http://www.auctionbytes.com) and its accompanying newsletters are favorites of ours—you'll find an astonishing amount of information here. The moderated forums run the gamut from general topics, such as fraud and marketing, to topics for collectors, such as books and glass. You can also sign up for two free email newsletters.

Auction Insights. Another excellent seller's resource, Auction Insights (http://www.auctioninsights.com) has a wealth of selling tips from PowerSellers, free auction tools, news, a message board, and links to related sites. You can also sign up for a free biweekly newsletter.

The Center for Help

eBay's Help Center covers virtually every aspect of buying, selling, searching, and otherwise using eBay. To display the Help Center, click the Help button at the top of nearly every eBay page.

To search for a term or phrase, such as *reserve auction*, type it here and then click Search Help.

Browse a book-like index of help subjects.

Wondering what MIB stands for? Check eBay's list of popular acronyms.

Contact eBay customer service. The process involves choosing categories that describe your question or problem, then typing the specifics. eBay claims it responds within 24 to 48 hours; we've had mixed results.

Browse this area for answers to eBay's most commonly asked questions.

Have a question? The Answer Center might hold the answer.

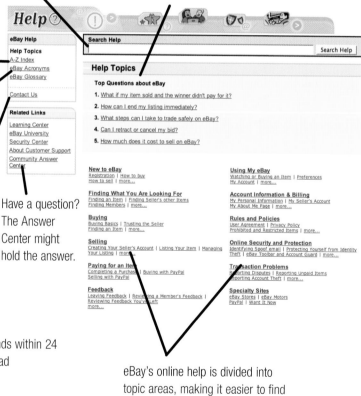

eBay's online help is divided into topic areas, making it easier to find the information you're looking for.

Live Help. Live Help lets you have a real-time, online conversation with an eBay support rep. We have found this feature to be rather useful. Look for the Live Help button on eBay's home page and elsewhere. Click it to display the Live Help window. Follow the directions, and you'll be chatting in no time.

Live Help

Helping hands. Throughout eBay's site are links that summon appropriate help pages. These helping hands are eBay's way of anticipating questions you might have while working your way through the site. Keep your eyes peeled for these helpful links—eBay often gives you the opportunity to learn more.

Get more HTML tips.

Protecting Your Account

Account and identify theft are real concerns to anyone doing business on the Internet today. Like most e-commerce sites, eBay takes precautions. In eBay's case, these precautions include requiring you to sign in as you navigate the site and making all its communications with you available in My eBay.

But there's no such thing as foolproof security, and the worst can and does happen. You've probably heard news reports about identity theft and credit card fraud in the eBay world. Honest eBayers have found themselves falling victim to thieves who hijack their good names, reputations, and credit.

On these and the following pages, you'll find some tips for protecting your account and some advice on what to do if you fear the worst.

Taking Precautions

The best offense is a good defense. Here's how to avoid becoming a victim to begin with.

Choose a unique User ID and password. As we mentioned on page 11, your User ID can't be an email address. This helps prevent the "harvesting" of your email address by would-be spammers who are looking to send you junk email.

Avoid using the same User ID for multiple Web sites—for example, don't make your eBay ID the same as your Amazon.com ID.

The same applies to passwords. Change your password regularly and avoid using words that can be found in a dictionary, or expressions that describe you in any way, such as *poodlegirl* or *shoeshopper*. This is a good policy when it comes to any important online account. You'll find more tips for choosing a password on page 10.

Don't fall for spoofs. You may receive an email that claims to be from eBay or PayPal asking you to update your account information. Don't fall for it. These so-called spoof emails are designed to get you to give up credit card numbers and other private information. They may look like official eBay or PayPal emails, and may even direct you to Web pages that look like eBay or PayPal pages. Don't go there.

eBay never asks you to provide sensitive information via email, never sends attachments, and never requires you to enter private information onto a page that is not directly connected to the eBay site.

If an email looks suspicious, don't click any of its links or open any attachments. (See page 30 for some tips on spotting a phony.) eBay recommends that you forward the email, complete with its Internet header information, to spoof@ebay.com. For details—and for advice from the source on how to tell a genuine eBay page from a phony—see www.ebay.com/help/confidence/isgw-account-theft-spoof.html.

Use virus-protection software. It pays to use virus-protection software, especially if you have a Windows computer. Viruses and worms can wreak havoc on your email program, spy on and record your keystrokes, and generally mess with your mind. Keep your virus software updated for maximum protection.

eBay Toolbar and Account Guard

If you're using Microsoft Internet Explorer and Microsoft Windows, eBay Toolbar is a handy add-on that helps you keep track of active listings and items you're watching, stay on top of important alerts, and perform eBay searches without having to go to eBay's site.

To download eBay Toolbar, go to http://pages.ebay.com/ ebay_toolbar. At this writing, eBay Toolbar works with Internet Explorer only, though eBay says it's working on compatibility with other Windows browsers.

From the account-protection standpoint, the most exciting feature of eBay Toolbar is Account Guard. It's a watchdog for you and your personal information, letting you know when you might be on a suspected or known spoof site.

How it works. If, heaven forbid, you click on a link in a spoof email or find your way to a site that eBay feels is suspicious, Account Guard's site indicator turns red. The indicator is green when you're at an eBay- or PayPal-verified site. Most of the time, the indicator is grey, meaning the site you are visiting has not been identified.

If you think there's some funny business going on, you can report the site to eBay through the Account Guard drop-down menu.

As you can see, the drop-down menu also serves as a gateway to many of eBay's important security features.

Guarding the door. You can also have eBay alert you when you attempt to enter your PayPal or eBay passwords into an unverified site. eBay Toolbar blocks you from submitting your password unless you confirm that you want to do so. This feature is meant to prevent you from giving your password to potential baddies, and to discourage you from using your eBay or PayPal passwords for other sites. (We join eBay in encouraging you to use different passwords for your various online accounts.)

Click the Alerts button to see all your eBay Alerts. Bidding on an item that's ending soon? Just been outbid? A small pop-up window containing a link to the item page appears in the bottom corner of your screen when an alert goes off.

Search eBay's listings whenever you like. Use the Search drop-down menu to narrow your search.

Account Guard changes color as you surf to indicate whether the site you're viewing is suspicious.

Pop over to My eBay with a single click.

Customize eBay Toolbar here.

Spotting a Spoof and Taking Action

Spotting a Spoof

Spoofers can mask their dirty deeds in a variety of ways. Here's one example.

eBay has published several resources relating to spoofing; the spoof-detection page we recommend on page 28 is the best place to learn about spoofing techniques. For a comprehensive tutorial about spoofs and how to avoid being victimized by them, see:

http://pages.ebay.com/ education/spooftutorial/

The eBay Security and Resolution Center is another good place to turn if you believe you have received or been victim of a spoof email:

http://pages.ebay.com/ securitycenter/index.html

It says it's from eBay, but it isn't. This information is easy to forge and graphics are easy to steal.

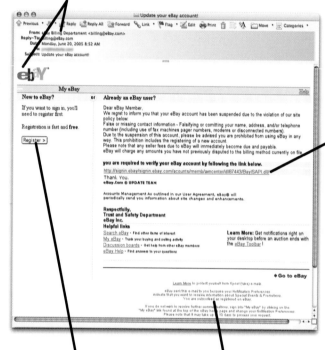

This link isn't real, either. Spoofers employ technical tricks to hide the actual addresses of their servers behind what appear to be authentic eBay URLs. Avoid clicking links in these types of emails. Although eBay may occasionally include a link in one of its emails, you can always copy that link and paste it into a new browser page. eBay will never ask you to submit sensitive information on a page linked from an email.

Don't take the bait! These thieves are trying to lure the unsuspecting reader to their site, where they will gather personal information for their own nefarious purposes.

These guys are good: they've even included a phony URL and a warning about spoofing.

Taking Action

If you fear you've fallen victim to a spoofer, there are some steps you can take.

Change your password immediately. Hopefully, you'll beat the baddies to the punch and they haven't already changed your password.

Change your secret question or password hint. When you created your eBay account, you specified a secret question and answer (see page 11). This enables you to retrieve your password if you forget it: answer this question and provide some additional account information, and eBay will email your password to you.

It's entirely likely that a lot of people know your mother's maiden name or the name of your first school. Consider choosing a false or misspelled answer to your question. (Make note of your incorrect answer so you aren't stumped yourself!)

To change your secret question, go to My eBay and in the My Account area, click the Personal Information link. In the User ID and Password Information section, click the Edit link next to Secret Question. You can then choose a different secret question (you won't be able to reuse the same secret question).

Contact your credit card company. If you provided a credit card number, cancel that card pronto. Your credit card company should be able to issue you a new card and number relatively quickly. For more information, see:

www.ebay.com/help/confidence/ problems-identity-theft.html

If you suspect someone has accessed or tried to access your account without your permission, spring into action before too much damage is done. To learn what steps you should take, see:

www.ebay.com/help/confidence/ isgw-account-theft-reporting.html

Using My eBay Messages

The best way to verify that a communication you receive from eBay is for real is to check the My Messages area in My eBay.

Whenever eBay sends you an email about your account—whether it's an account status notice, an invoice, or a question from another eBayer—a copy of that message also appears in your My Messages Inbox. If you're uncertain about whether an email is for real, check this area of My eBay to see if it appears here, too.

Use the folders eBay has created for you, peruse messages you've sent, or create new folders to file your messages from eBay (and other eBay members) here.

Only eBay itself sends alerts, which are important communications that typically require your immediate attention. You can't delete an alert until you have acted on it or at least read it.

You can expect to find many other types of missives in your My Messages area: messages from other eBay users, questions about active listings, and, perhaps, Second Chance offers.

To learn more about My Messages, see:

http://pages.ebay.com/help/ myebay/my-messages.html

31

CHAPTER 2

Creating an Auction

Listing an Item: The Big Picture

Creating an auction listing is a multi-step process. We'll be detailing each step in this chapter of the book, but before we do, let's step back and look at the big picture with this overview of the listing process.

And remember, before you start creating a listing, do your homework: verify that your item is allowed, search completed auctions to see how similar items have fared, and perform the other pre-auction steps we outlined in the previous chapter.

The steps behind creating an auction change from time to time, as eBay evolves its site and adds new selling features. As we were working on this revised edition, eBay was working on a new set of procedures for creating an auction. For a look at this new listing-creation process, see Appendix D. And remember, you'll find updates on this book's companion Web site, www.ebaymatters.com.

Choose a Selling Format

Choose between a conventional online auction, a fixed-price sale, and other options (page 37).

Select a Category

Many eBay buyers browse by category—choosing the right category can help people find your item (page 36).

Create a Title and Description

A well-crafted title will help attract buyers who use eBay's search features. Once you've attracted them, reel them in with an honest, thorough, and tantalizing description (page 38).

Optional: Specify Item Specifics

For some categories, including music recordings and concert tickets, you can provide extra details that can help searchers (page 39) find what they're looking for.

Specify Duration and Pricing

When should your auction start and low long should it last? And what's your starting price? These details can affect bidding—and your bottom line (page 40).

Sell Your Item: Enter Pictures & Item Details

1. Category 2. Title & Description 3. Pictures & Details 4. Payment & Shipping

Title
Kill The Man (Luke Wilson/Joshua Malina), NIB. DVD

Pricing and duration

Price your item competitively to increase your chance of a successful sale.

NEW! Get ideas about pricing by searching completed items...

Starting price *Required
$ |

A lower starting price can encourage more bids.

Buy It Now price (Fee Varies)
$ |

Reserve price (fee varies)
$ |

Specify Item Location

Where are you? Buyers need this information because your location can affect shipping costs significantly.

Item location

ZIP Code: 95466
Location display: Philo, California United States
Change

Prepare and Add Photos

It's hard to imagine buying something sight unseen—give your bidders some virtual face time with your item (page 42).

Add pictures
Use these tips to add a great photo to your listing.

eBay Basic Picture Services | Your Web hosting

Picture 1 (Free)
[   ] Browse...

To add pictures to your listing, click Browse.

Optional: Add Frills

An ever-expanding array of options can make your auction more visible, attractive, and expensive to create (page 46).

Provide Payment and Shipping Details

Specify your payment requirements, who will pay for shipping, destinations you're willing to serve, and more (pages 50-55).

Payment methods
Choose the payment methods you'll accept from buyers.

PayPal
[MasterCard] [VISA] [AMEX] [DISCOVER] [eCheck]

PayPal allows you to accept credit card payments in multiple currencies from buyers in 45 countries worldwide.

You have opted to offer PayPal for all your listings. Edit preferences

✓ PayPal payment notification will go to: [   ]
Edit preferences
No account needed. Fees may apply.

Other payment methods
☑ Money Order / Cashier's Check
☐ Personal Check
☐ Other / See Item Description

Review and Submit

All the details of your auction appear on one page. Proofread the text, fix problems, and when everything looks good, submit your auction and wait for the bids (page 56).

Selecting a Category

In a department store, people tend to shop in one of two ways: they approach a sales clerk and ask for a specific item, or they wander into an interesting department and start browsing.

eBay shopping works similarly. Potential bidders can ask for a specific item by conducting a search, or they can wander into a particular category and start browsing.

Categories are akin to the departments in a store, and one of the first steps in creating an auction listing is to choose a category for your item. The more specific you can be, the better your chance of turning browsers into bidders.

And you can be mighty specific. eBay has thousands of categories, the most popular of which are listed on eBay's home page. To see even more, go to www.ebay.com/buy, where you can explore the thousands of subcategories that serve to classify the entirety of human endeavor. Or at least a hefty chunk of it.

But you don't have to explore every category to find the right one. With the techniques described here, you can home in on the right category quickly.

Finding the right category isn't just a good idea—it's a rule. If eBay spies an inappropriately categorized item, it may move the listing into a more appropriate category. And if you list something belonging in the Mature Audiences category anywhere else, eBay will end that listing.

Strategies for Categories

Not sure where to park your item? Search for similar items to see what other sellers have done. Use search keywords appropriate to your auction, ones you're likely to use in your auction's title (page 84). Examine successful completed auctions that are similar to yours and note their categories, which appear near the top of the auction page.

Finding Categories

The appearance of the Choose a Category page varies depending on several factors, including what computer and browser you're using. We've encountered several versions of the page, and aren't convinced that we've seen them all.

All of the variants have some common ground: they all allow you to search for categories by typing keywords that describe your item or by browsing eBay's directory of categories. If you see a version of the page that differs from what's printed here, just apply these concepts to the version that eBay decided you should see.

One common version of the page appears below.

How have other sellers categorized items similar to yours? To find out, type some words that describe your item and then click Search for Categories. A list of categories appears (opposite page). **Note:** In some versions of the Choose a Category page, this box is labeled *Enter keywords to find a category.*

The whole shebang: You can browse eBay's category directory using a browser similar to the one on the opposite page.

Selling something similar to an item that you've already sold? Click to display a list of categories you've used recently. **Note:** Some versions of the Choose a Category page don't provide a link to recently used categories.

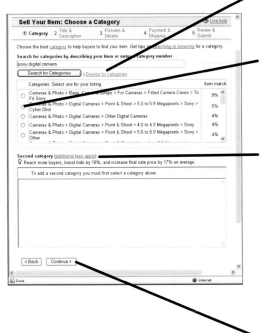

Browse eBay's category directory (at right).

Categories corresponding to the keywords you typed appear here. Scroll through the list to find the category that seems most appropriate to your item, then select it by clicking the button to its left.

A second category? You've decided to retire that beautiful ceramic dog bowl. Should it go under Pottery or Pet Supplies? If you just can't decide, you can list your item in two categories. Doing so doubles your insertion fees and any listing upgrades. Is a second category worth the cost? We think doing thorough research and following the lead of successful completed auctions is far more fruitful.

All done? When you've finished specifying categories, click Continue.

Browsing Categories

If you'd rather browse eBay's available categories instead of relying on what previous sellers have done, you can use the category browser. While its workings can also differ depending on your computer and browser, its basics are the same: you can choose a main category and then drill down into the appropriate subcategory.

Choosing Your Selling Format

Before you get to the category selection screens we've shown here, you must choose what kind of format your auction will take. We've stashed this information here because in the vast majority of cases, you'll be using the classic *online auction* format, where your listing col-

lects bids and your item goes to the highest bidder.

Two other options are for *fixed-price* auctions and for real estate. In a fixed-price auction, no bidding takes place. Set a price for your item, and if someone agrees to pay it, the auction ends. Your listings still

appear in a specific category, as with conventional auctions.

Note: This option appears only if you have a feedback rating of at least 10, or if you go through the ID Verified process on page 13. If you have a PayPal account or accept PayPal payments, you only need a feedback rating of 5.

As for the real estate format, think of it as a classified ad for your property. Interested buyers fill out a contact form and the information is sent to you. This format is really more of a lead-generation mechanism than an auction.

Describe Your Item: Title and Description

After you choose a category for your item, it's time to put on your copywriter's hat and work through the Title and Description screen. At this stage, your job is to create a title that will snag searchers and entice them to click through to your auction's page, and to write a description that inspires them to bid.

You might also dip your toe into the waters of Web design, adding formatting codes that improve the appearance of your item's description—by using different text sizes and type fonts, for example.

What should you put in your title? How should you format your description? And what should you write? We'll answer these questions in detail later. Our focus at this stage is to look at mechanics of the Title & Description page to see how it works.

This page is one of the few pages on eBay that works differently depending on whether you're using a Windows computer or a Macintosh. Even within Windows, the page's operation can differ depending on which browser you use. If you use the latest versions of Internet Explorer for Windows, you can take advantage of a useful tool, called the HTML editor, which eBay has created for formatting the text of your descriptions.

If you use a different browser—or a Mac— the HTML editor is not available to you, and you must format your descriptions manually by typing codes. Not to worry—it isn't all that difficult, and we'll show you how later.

This area shows where you are in the process of creating a listing. To backtrack to a specific step, click its link.

Creating an effective title means mastering the art of *keywords*— the terms that shoppers type into eBay's Search box. For titling tips, see page 84.

Add an item subtitle using this listing option, which costs 50 cents. A subtitle is another opportunity to entice a potential bidder to view your listing (see page 85).

Using the HTML Text Editor

HTML stands for *hypertext markup language*, and it's the set of codes used to control the formatting of Web pages. It isn't difficult to learn the handful of HTML codes that are most commonly used in eBay descriptions, and indeed, we've devoted pages 86 to 89 to the subject. But if you use Microsoft Windows and version 6 or later of the Internet Explorer browser, you can also use eBay's HTML editor to control formatting.

When you click the Standard link (circled on the opposite page), your browser makes the Standard tab active. This window resembles the standard item description tab, but look closely—you'll see a set of word processor-like toolbars above the Item Description box.

Use the upper toolbar to choose fonts, sizes, colors, type style and alignment, and to create numbered or bulleted lists and indents.

If you have boilerplate text you use often in your auctions—and if you use Microsoft Windows and the Internet Explorer browser—you can use Inserts to help save you some time and typing; see page 83.

To preview your description, click this link. A new browser window appears containing the description, complete with any formatting you've specified.

When you're happy with your title and description, click Continue.

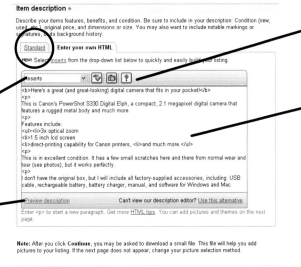

Use this toolbar to check spelling, add a photo, or get help.

Here's where you provide the information potential buyers need to determine whether your item is for them. To apply simple formatting to your text, you can type HTML codes (such as <p>, which begins a new paragraph). For details on writing a great description, see page 85. For the lowdown on formatting and HTML, see pages 86–89.

Special Options: Pre-filled Information and Item Specifics

Depending on what you're selling, you may want to take advantage of some special description options that eBay provides.

Pre-filled item information. With many categories—for example, consumer electronics, books, music CDs, and DVDs—eBay provides a head start for describing your item. With *pre-filled item information,* eBay lets you automatically retrieve information—a camera's specifications, a book's author, a CD's list of songs—by choosing options from

pop-up menus or by typing a product code printed on the item.

Pre-filled item information often includes stock photography that you can add to your auction. If you're selling something whose vital statistics are already in eBay's vast product database, you can take advantage of that information to provide more details and cut down on typing.

But don't rely exclusively on pre-filled item information. It's also a good idea to supplement the information eBay provides with at least a couple of sentences about your specific

item: "This book is in great condition but the dust jacket is torn." And consider taking your own photos, especially of items that have visible wear that buyers will want to know about.

If pre-filled information is available for the category you've chosen, you'll see the options for retrieving the information when you click Continue after choosing the category. If you're curious to see how pre-filled information works, just start a new auction and choose one of the types of categories we mentioned previously, such as books.

Item specifics. For some item categories, the Title & Description page includes an additional area, Item Specifics, where you can specify details about your item by checking boxes and choosing options from menus. Potential bidders can search for these criteria. Not all categories provide these additional options, and in most of those that do, you aren't required to fill them out. But we recommend doing so—it can only help your cause to describe your item as precisely as possible.

Pictures and Details: Getting Specific

You've chosen a category and written your title and description. Now it's time to specify key details about the auction itself, such as its duration, starting time, starting price, and reserve price, if any. Your choices at this stage can affect the closing price of your auction and even have an influence on your seller's fees.

You specify these details using the Pictures and Details page. This page also contains options for adding photos to your auction and for dressing up your listing with various design templates. We'll focus on the photos and other eye-candy options in the pages to come.

How Long an Auction?

Auctions normally run for seven days, but with the Duration pop-up menu, you can specify a duration of one day, three days, five days, or ten days.

Tip: Whichever duration you choose, try to run your auction over the course of a weekend to increase the number of potential bidders. A seven-day auction ensures that your listing will span a weekend.

If you have a time-sensitive item (such as concert tickets), a one- or three-day auction makes sense. A five-day duration is a good way to keep bidders interested and bring in the cash a bit sooner. A ten-day auction gives bidders more time to bid your item up, but your auction may go stale after a week. Bidders may lose interest—or find something else to buy. And it'll cost you an extra 40 cents.

Clock Watching: Timing Your Auctions

Timing may not be everything, but it's an important thing on eBay. An auction's success can be influenced by when it ends—if an auction ends during prime Web-surfing time, you stand a better chance of having a last-minute bidding war that will drive up your closing price.

Start time. As we mention on the opposite page, an auction begins when you click the Submit button on the Review & Submit page. If you choose a five-day duration and submit your listing on Friday at 11:52 a.m., the auction will end at 11:52 a.m. the following Wednesday.

When is the best time to start an auction? The real question is, when is the best time for an auction to *end?* Opinions vary, but we think evenings are best. Folks are home from work and parked at their computers, ready to surf and snipe and bid and buy.

Other sellers prefer to have an auction end during work hours—to snare people who surf on their employers' high-speed lines. But agreement is universal that the worst time for an auction to end is in the middle of the night.

And when is the best *day* to end an auction? Research indicates that Sunday evening is the best time for auctions to end. At the very least, time your auctions so they don't end on a Friday evening or Saturday, a holiday, or a holiday weekend.

Scheduling a start time. To time your auction's close with precision, pay an extra 10 cents and schedule the auction to start at a specific time, up to three weeks in advance. That way, you can compose an auction in the middle of the night or when you're on the road but still have it end at an optimum time. For example, if you're going to be in transit on Monday and Tuesday and unable to answer bidder questions, simply have the auction start on Wednesday.

Official eBay time. eBay operates on Pacific time. If you aren't in the Pacific time zone, do the math when you specify your auction's start time. Also note that eBay auction pages list time in 24-hour format: for example, 1:15 p.m. is listed as 13:15.

Where to begin? See pages 18–21 for advice on determining the potential value of your item and strategies for setting your starting price.

Adding a Buy It Now price to your auction allows a bidder to buy your item at that price and immediately end the auction. Once someone bids on your item, the Buy It Now option disappears and the auction continues normally. See page 21 for the pros and cons of this feature.

Note: Buy It Now isn't available until you have a feedback rating of at least 10 (5, if you accept PayPal) or have been ID Verified (see page 13).

You can donate a portion of your proceeds to charity. Learn more about eBay Giving Works at http://pages.ebay.com/help/sell/selling-nonprofit.html#6.

Pricing and duration

Price your item competitively to increase your chance of a successful sale.

NEW! Get ideas about pricing by searching completed items...

Starting price *Required
$9.99
A lower starting price can encourage more bids.

Reserve price (fee varies)
$
The lowest price at which you're willing to sell your item is the reserve price.

Buy It Now price (Fee Varies)
$
Sell to the first buyer who meets your Buy It Now price.

NEW! **Donate percentage of sale**
No nonprofit selected ▼   Select % ▼
If you choose to participate in this program and your item sells, a $10 minimum donation is required (does not apply to nonprofits selling on their own behalf). Learn more about eBay Giving Works.

Duration *
7 days ▼
When to use a 1-day duration.

Private listing
Allow your buyers to remain anonymous to other eBay users. Learn when to use private listings.
☐ Private listing.

Start time
◉ Start listing when submitted
○ Schedule start time ($0.10) Select a date... ▼ Select a time... ▼ PDT
Learn more about scheduled listings.

Quantity *
| Individual Items | Lots |

Quantity *
1
Learn more about multiple item listings.

Selling similar or identical items together in a "lot"?
Help buyers find your listing - just enter the number of items you have in the Lots tab above.

Item location
ZIP Code: 95466
Location display: Philo, California United States
Change

With large, heavy, or fragile items, location can be everything. A cheap grand piano isn't so grand if shipping costs are exorbitant, and a bargain-priced vase is no bargain if it arrives in smithereens. To avoid problems like these, many buyers search for items located in regions close to them. Accurate location information is critical for these folks.

Chances are you're selling just one of whatever you're listing. But if you have an entire cache of Village People charm bracelets to unload, you can also create a multiple-item auction (also called a *Dutch auction*). Get the details at www.ebay.com/help/sell/multiple.html.

Note: To create a multiple-item auction, you must either have a feedback rating of at least 30 and be a registered member for at least two weeks, or be ID Verified (page 13).

You can specify a "secret" price that represents the minimum you're willing to accept. If that price isn't met, your auction ends without a winning bidder and you're protected from selling your item for less than you feel it's worth. We don't recommend setting a reserve price; see page 21.

Your bidders' User IDs aren't displayed on the listing or history pages. Once the auction ends, only you will know the winning bidder's ID. You might choose this option for auctions whose bidders want to remain anonymous. (Use your imagination.)

Normally, an auction begins when you click the Submit button on the Review and Submit page. But for an extra 10 cents, you can schedule an auction to start at a different time. For details, see the sidebar on the previous page.

Worth a Thousand Words: Adding Pictures

Pictures are critical to most eBay auctions. In fact, they're so important that we've devoted an entire chapter of this book to auction photography. Chapter 3 covers the tools, lighting and composition techniques, and software you can use to make your eBay pictures look their best. Here, we focus (sorry about that) on the steps involved in adding pictures to your listing.

Most eBay sellers use eBay Picture Services to add pictures to their auctions. As the name says, eBay Picture Services is provided by eBay itself: you use the Pictures & Details page to add photos to your listing, and eBay stores the photos and formats them into your listing.

eBay Picture Services allows up to twelve pictures on a listing page. One photo is free; each additional photo costs 15 cents at this writing. You can also buy some picture upgrades, such as slide shows and big, supersized pictures that are great for showing details.

The alternative to using eBay Picture Services is to store your auction photos elsewhere—to host them yourself, either on a Web server if you have access to one, or using a picture-hosting service. This alternative is more complicated, but has some advantages that we discuss on the opposite page.

If you haven't taken your photos yet, read through Chapter 3, then snap those shots and prepare them as described on page 78. Then return to this page to learn how to add photos to your listing.

Enhanced versus Basic Picture Services

eBay Picture Services comes in two flavors: Basic and Enhanced. If you're running Microsoft Windows and using Internet Explorer version 4.0 or later, you can use Enhanced Picture Services. It provides more features, including the ability to make minor tweaks to your images before adding them to your auction.

Most significantly, Enhanced Picture Services automatically makes your pictures the proper size to fit into eBay's listing format and transfer quickly, even over slow Internet connections. This eliminates the extra step of using digital-imaging software to downsize your pictures before transferring them to eBay.

If you're using a Macintosh computer—or a Windows computer running the Netscape or Firefox browsers or a very old version of Internet Explorer—you can't use the enhanced version. Instead, you'll use Basic Picture Services. Don't feel left out; you aren't missing all that much, and we'll describe the differences as we go along.

A short download. To use eBay Enhanced Picture Services, you must allow the download of a small (and free) software program. If you're running Windows and a recent version of Internet Explorer, click the Enhanced Picture Services tab on the Pictures & Details page. Next, click the Set Up Picture Services button.

When installation begins, a security warning appears asking if you'd like to install eBay Enhanced Picture Control. To proceed with the installation, click the Install button. If you click Don't Install, you won't be able to use Enhanced Picture Services.

After you've installed Enhanced Picture Control, you can skip on to page 44 for a look at how to use it.

Hosting Your Own Pictures

eBay Picture Services is easy to use and provides a versatile assortment of formatting options. So why bother hosting your own pictures?

Cost cutting. eBay charges extra when you add more than one photo to a listing, and it charges even more if you want large images. If you already have access to a Web server, you can save on listing fees by hosting your own pictures. If you create many auctions and like to provide big, detail-filled images, the savings will add up quickly.

Formatting flexibility. eBay Picture Services lets you put images anywhere you want, as long as it's at the bottom of a listing page. You might prefer to scatter images throughout your listing page. Hosting your own pictures makes this possible. You have to learn some additional HTML formatting codes, but they aren't difficult (see page 89).

A host of options. Finally, hosting your own images gives you freedoms that eBay Picture Services doesn't provide. You can reuse photos in future auctions without having to upload (and pay for) them again. You can use photos with unusual dimensions— for example, very wide or very tall—instead of being locked into eBay Picture Services' postcard-like proportions. And with a tip we share on page 73, you can change photos after an auction has started, even if bids have already come in. (As described on page 96, you can't change photos on an auction that has bids.)

Are You Being Served?

A *Web server* is a computer that transmits text and graphics (among other things) to other computers over the Internet. When you visit a Web site, your browser is communicating with a server.

You may have access to a server and not know it. Many Internet providers give their subscribers a small amount of space on their vast servers. You can use this server space to create your own home page— or to store and serve your auction photos.

Contact your Internet provider and ask if your subscription includes server space, and if so, if you can host auction photos. (Some providers prohibit photo hosting because dishing out large images can bog down their servers.) If you strike gold, you'll have some technicalities to learn; they're summarized on pages 78 and 89. If you strike out, don't give up. Several free or inexpensive image hosting services are available. Examples include easypichost. com, freepicturehosting.com, and andale. com. See page 148 for more information.

With many image hosting services, you transfer pictures by using your Web browser. If you'll be hosting your pictures through an Internet provider such as Earthlink, you may need an FTP program to transfer the pictures to the server. (FTP stands for *file-transfer protocol*.) For Windows, we recommend CuteFTP (www.cuteftp.com). On the Mac, we're fond of Transmit (www.panic.com).

More Photo Flexibility with eBay Picture Manager

With eBay's extra-cost Picture Manager service, you can eliminate many of the drawbacks of eBay Picture Services without having to deal with the complexities of hosting photos yourself.

With Picture Manager, you can add multiple photos to each of your auctions without having to pay the 15 cents eBay normally charges for each additional photo. You can reuse photos in multiple auctions without having to upload them again and again.

You can have your User ID printed on your pictures to help guard against photo theft (see page 72). You can manage a library of photos using My eBay. And you can place photos within a listing description instead of relegating them to the bottom of the page.

A subscription to Picture Manager starts at $9.99 per month for 50MB of storage. To learn more, see www.ebay. com/picturemanager.

Using eBay Picture Services

Step 1.
Prep Your Photos

Using Chapter 3 as your guide, take the required photos, fine-tune them as needed, and downsize them for the Web. **Note:** If you intend to use Enhanced Picture Services, don't resize your photos beforehand.

Tip: If this auction will have more than one photo, consider stashing all the photos in their own folder—this will make it easier to locate them later.

Step 2.
Choose the Photos

Use the Add Pictures portion of the Pictures & Details page to transfer your photos and choose layout options.

You can switch between Enhanced and Basic Picture Services.

Rotate, crop, and fine-tune a picture (see page 75).

Hosting your own photos? Click this link (see "Hosting Your Own?" on the opposite page).

To add a picture, click Add Pictures. An Open dialog box appears. Locate the picture, double-click its name, and the picture appears. Repeat for each picture you want to add, but remember that only the first picture is free.

To remove a picture, click Remove Pictures. To remove multiple pictures, Shift-click on each one before clicking this button.

You can choose from a variety of extra-cost layout and presentation options. See Step 3 for details.

Basic Picture Services

Before using Basic Picture Services to add pictures, resize them according to the directions on page 79.

To add a picture, click the Browse button. In the Open dialog box that appears, locate and double-click the picture you want to add.

The picture's file name and location on your hard drive will appear here. To remove a picture, drag across this information and then press the Delete key. To replace a picture, click the Browse button again and then choose a new photo.

Note: When using Basic eBay Picture Services, you can't transfer any file larger than 2MB. If you follow the instructions on page 79, your photos will be much smaller than this, so this isn't a serious limitation.

Step 3 (optional).
Add Picture Layout
Options

Depending on what you're selling, you might find these extra-cost picture layout options useful.

In the Standard layout, you can have up to twelve photos, which appear near the bottom of the listing page as shown below. A small version of the first photo also appears at the top of the listing page.

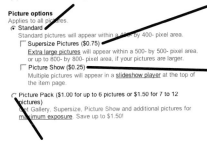

A combination platter of picture options: you get a Gallery photo (see page 47), Supersize pictures, and six pictures. At this writing, it's $1.75 worth of upgrades for $1.

The Standard Picture Layout

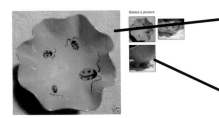

The first picture you add appears in its full-size glory.

When you add more than one picture, every picture has a small thumbnail version. When a viewer clicks on a thumbnail, its picture replaces the larger picture on the left.

Bidders can click on a picture and see a larger, more detailed version. A Supersize picture must be at least 500 by 500 pixels, and can be up to 800 by 800 pixels (see page 79).

Use up to twelve images to create an interactive slideshow (below). Potential bidders can stop, start, advance, or reverse the show. It's a nice way to show your object from multiple angles.

Step 4.
Finish Up and Move On

The lower portion of the Pictures & Details page contains listing upgrades that we cover on the following pages. When you've added the upgrades (or skipped past them) and are ready to move on, click the Continue button at the bottom of the page.

Hosting Your Own?

If you're hosting photos yourself, click the Your Web Hosting tab.

If you've added <img> tags to your item description, check this box so that eBay will display the picture icon ( ) alongside your item in search-results pages, if you don't choose the Gallery photo option.

If you're hosting only one photo for this auction, enter its Web address here. If you're hosting more than one photo for this auction, add HTML <img> tags to your item description (see page 89).

To create a picture show from self-hosted photos, check this box to display an area where you can type the addresses of the pictures.

45

The Frills: Listing Options

Scattered throughout the Pictures & Details page, you'll find a selection of extra-cost options that you can add to your listing. And we'll be upfront with you: most of these options are gimmicks that will help eBay's bottom line more than yours.

Having said that, though, there are some genuinely useful options here. Some upgrades provide auction flexibility, such as the ability to start an auction at a specific time or to create a Buy It Now auction. These are inexpensive upgrades that make a lot of sense for some auctions, and we elaborate on them on page 21.

Other options are designed to help your listing stand out from the competition. For example, the Gallery upgrade displays a small image of your item in the search-results page. We're big fans of this upgrade, which costs a mere 35 cents.

Some listing upgrades are much pricier. For $19.95, you can get the Featured Plus! upgrade—your listing will show up in the Featured area that appears at the top of the listing page for your chosen category and search-results pages. And for a whopping $39.95, your listing appears at the top of the main listings page and maybe (although eBay offers no guarantees) in the Featured area of the eBay home page.

When it comes to listing upgrades, our advice is to run the numbers. Before you add extra doodads to your listing, calculate their price, also factoring in the requisite insertion and final value fees. Be sure the earning potential of your auction is commensurate with what you're spending to create it.

Listing Designer

For an extra ten cents, you can clutter up the description area of your listing with any of more than 200 design themes. The themes range from hokey to festively hokey.

To see a small preview of a template, select a theme and choose a design from the list below.

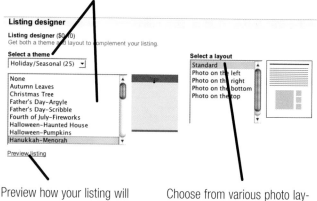

Preview how your listing will look with its makeover.

Choose from various photo layouts. You don't have to choose a theme in order to choose a different photo layout.

The main reason we dislike these themes isn't because of their design—it's because adding visual gewgaws to a listing page increases its download time. Browsing on eBay is slow enough as it is. Why make things worse?

Until eBay publishes statistics proving that strollers sell for higher amounts when their listings are wearing the Baby theme, we say keep it simple. Let a great description and great photos do the selling.

Page Counters

Curious about how many people are viewing your auction page? It's easy to find out: add a page counter to the bottom of the page. And unlike most of the other listing upgrades discussed here, page counters are free.

The *page counter* is a digital odometer that shows how many times your listing has been viewed. This can give you an idea of the demand for your item, as well as how good a job you're doing writing titles and descriptions.

Page counter
- ○ No counter
- ● **1234** Andale Style
- ○ **1234** Green LED
- ○ Thanks for looking! Hidden (Only you see page views)

To hide or not to hide? That is the question. If your viewers know that there is plenty of interest in your item, they may feel more compelled to bid right away. However, if you want to play it close to the vest, you can keep your potential bidders guessing by choosing Hidden.

To learn more about Andale counters and viewing statistics for all your auctions, see page 105.

Preview Your Upgrade

Beneath the Listing Designer area is a preview that shows you what your listing will look like when it appears on a search-results page. Above and below the preview of your listing are other upgrade examples.

Here's what our listing, with Gallery and Highlight upgrade options added, will look like on a search-results page.

A Field Guide to Listing Upgrades

Here's a quick reference guide to more of the upgrades you'll find on the Pictures & Details page.

Option	Cost	Comments
Featured Plus!	$19.95	Your listing appears toward the top of the listing page for your chosen category and resulting search pages.
Home Page Featured	$39.95	This option buys prime real estate: your listing appears at the top of the main listings page and maybe, just maybe, in the Featured area of eBay's home page.
Highlight	$5.00	Sets your listing apart with a colorful background. This one is a bit pricier than it's worth. New Coach Signature cell phone case, gray/white NR
Bold	$1.00	Emphasizes your auction link by formatting it in bold. **New Coach Signature cell phone case, gray/white NR**
Gallery	$0.35	Displays a small image of your item in the search-results page, enabling potential bidders to see the item and, hopefully, enticing them to view your listing. We're big fans of this feature. New Coach Signature cell phone case, gray/white NR
Gift Services	$0.25	To add this option and its nifty icon to your listing, you must offer any of the gift services eBay suggests: gift wrapping/card, express shipping, or shipping directly to the gift recipient.

47

Shipping: Exploring Your Options

The topic of shipping is so important that we're taking a break from the auction-creation process to focus on it.

There are couriers and carriers of all kinds, but most eBay shipments make their journey by way of the United States Postal Service, United Parcel Service, or FedEx.

Here's an overview of the shipping options we find most useful. You can find more information and shipping tips at eBay's Shipping Center, www.ebay.com/services/buyandsell/shipping.html.

As you survey your shipping options, you'll need to consider several factors. How fast does your shipment need to get there? FedEx is fast, but it isn't cheap. Do you need insurance? Some carriers give you more than others. Do you need tracking numbers and delivery confirmation notices? Some carriers charge extra for them.

You may end up using a combination of these carriers and maybe some we haven't listed here. Use the carrier that provides the best mix of fast delivery, low cost, and extra services such as tracking. And if its drop-off location is on your way to work, so much the better.

US Postal Service

www.usps.com

Pros: Post offices are everywhere; competitive rates; extensive free supplies; delivers to street addresses or post office boxes.

Cons: Overnight service can be spotty; tracking, insurance, and confirmation often cost extra.

The US Postal Service (USPS) is the shipper of choice for most eBay sellers, particularly when shipping items that weigh under four pounds to US destinations. The USPS also has an excellent Web site where you can create labels, order supplies, and much more. For a complete directory of USPS mailing services and options, see www.usps.com/send. For current rate information, see www.usps.com/common/category/postage.htm.

Priority Mail is the gold standard for eBay shipments. Packages typically arrive within two to three days, Sundays excluded. Delivery time isn't guaranteed, however, so don't stake your reputation on that timeframe. If you print your shipping label online, you can get Delivery Confirmation service for free; see page 127.

Priority Mail service is available to every US address that has postal delivery service, including post office boxes and military addresses. The flat rate to ship a package that weighs up to one pound anywhere in the US, as of this writing, is $3.85. (Needless to say, all the rates we quote here will go up.) You can use your own packaging or the Priority Mail flat-rate envelope or boxes.

Express Mail is the USPS's fastest service, providing overnight delivery to most addresses nationwide, 365 days a year, including holidays and Sundays. If you or your recipient live in a rural area, expect two-day rather than overnight service, and don't expect holiday or Sunday delivery. Priority Mail tends to be a better, more economical choice for the boondocks.

An Express Mail package is automatically insured for $100. Express Mail also provides tracking number and proof-of-delivery services. Rates begin at about $10.40 for a package weighing eight ounces or less—pricey indeed.

First-Class Mail is the way a standard piece of mail travels. As with Priority Mail, delivery time is typically two to three days. You can use First-Class Mail for packages weighing 13 ounces or less. First-Class Mail can be more economical for lightweight items.

Media Mail is an excellent option for items such as books, printed music, CDs, DVDs, videotapes, and similar forms of media. Media Mail is slow—delivery time is typically seven to nine days—but inexpensive: $1.12 for the first pound and 42 cents for each additional pound. If you're shipping media and your buyer is willing to wait, Media Mail is an economical choice.

United Parcel Service

www.ups.com

Pros: Serves even the remotest areas; $100 insurance included in all shipments; accepts packages up to 150 pounds; free supplies when you create an account.

Cons: Can be costlier than USPS; extra charge for pickup service and delivery confirmation; delivers to street addresses only.

Where there's an eBay seller, there's often a brown truck, and for good reasons. UPS provides a full range of delivery options, detailed tracking, guaranteed delivery times, and $100 of insurance for each package. UPS also has an ever-increasing number of retail outlets and drop-off

locations nationwide, even in the sticks. As residents of Teeny Tiny America, we can attest to the fact that UPS is happy to find those of us who are not easily found.

Another plus: you can access the UPS site via the eBay Shipping Center, and eBay's shipping calculator provides comparison shopping between the Postal Service and UPS.

UPS is also an excellent choice for shipping the big stuff—where the US Postal Service maxes out at 70 pounds, UPS will take a package that weighs up to 150 pounds.

Here are the services we use most often.

3 Day Select service provides a nice balance between economy and reliability. Three-day delivery to any address in the 48 contiguous states is guaranteed, and tracking information is available.

2nd Day Air is pricier but faster, and also provides guaranteed two-day delivery to Hawaii, Puerto Rico, and Alaska (remote Alaskan locales may take longer).

UPS Ground is inexpensive but slower, typically taking two to five business days, depending on how far you're shipping.

UPS provides pickup services to many residential locations. You'll pay extra for pickup unless you schedule a daily pickup. Delivery confirmation costs an additional $1, but can be worth it.

To estimate shipping costs using various UPS services, use the UPS Quick Cost Calculator at wwwapps.ups.com/QCCWebApp/request?loc=en_US.

FedEx

www.fedex.com

Pros: Reliable overnight and rush services; free packing materials; accepts packages up to 150 pounds.

Cons: Tends to be costlier than the other two; delivers to street addresses only.

We tend to use FedEx only when sending overnight packages.

FedEx Express is the service to use if your buyer wants it now—and is willing to pay for it. Overnight, two-day, and three-day options are available, and even same-day service is available in some areas. Packages can weigh up to 150 pounds, and delivery is available Monday through Friday, with Saturday delivery available for an additional fee.

FedEx Ground Home Delivery is designed to compete with UPS and the Postal Service. Delivery to any residential address in the US takes up to five days within the Lower 48, and up to seven days to or from Alaska and Hawaii. (For delivery to business addresses, you must use FedEx Ground.) Maximum package weight is 70 pounds. Learn more at www.fedex.com/us/services/ground/us/homedelivery.

Payment and Shipping Details

Once you've described your item in detail, it's time to tell all about your payment requirements and shipping policies. The Payment & Shipping page is the place where you list these critical details.

Before you start choosing options and clicking check boxes, you need to make some decisions. What forms of payment will you accept? Will you or your buyer pay for shipping? Will you specify shipping costs ahead of time? Will the shipping fee be based on the buyer's location or will it be a flat fee? And will you require insurance? We'll help you answer these questions in the pages that follow.

If you have the same payment and shipping policies for most or all of your auctions, you'll be glad to know you don't have to specify these details manually every time you create a listing. eBay remembers the last payment and shipping details you specified; the next time you create an auction, those settings will already be made for you when you arrive at the Payment & Shipping page. (You can change the settings if you want, of course.)

What's more, if you'd like to automate the process of invoicing your customers and informing them of your payment requirements, you can use eBay's Checkout feature as described on page 53.

Payment Methods: Receiving Your Due

You can choose from a variety of payment methods, each with pros and cons (page 54). For example, personal checks demand patience and a bit more effort but don't cost you any money, while PayPal is fast and convenient but demands a share of your take.

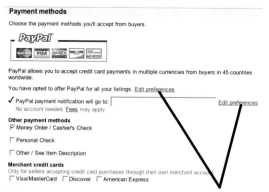

Edit your payment preferences and checkout preferences (page 53).

Buyer Financing Options

PayPal makes it possible for buyers to buy now and pay later with the PayPal Buyer Credit program. For an additional fee, PayPal will pay you in full, but allow your buyer to make monthly payments. For more info, go to http://pages.ebay.com/help/sell/ppbuyercredit.html.

Ship-To Locations: Where in the World?

Use this area to specify where you're willing to ship. If you're selling something particularly large or heavy, you may choose not to ship at all and only arrange local pickup with your buyer. In that case, click the button labeled *Will not ship - local pickup only*. For a look at the pros and cons (and the nuts and bolts) of serving the world, see page 130.

Ship-to locations *Required

⦿ Will ship to the United States and the following (check all that apply):
Reach more buyers - learn more about shipping internationally

☐ Worldwide   ☐ N. and S. America   ☐ Europe   ☐ Asia
          ☐ Canada   ☐ United Kingdom   ☐ Australia
          ☐ Mexico   ☐ Germany   ☐ Japan

○ Will not ship - local pickup only
Specify pickup arrangements in the Payment Instructions box below.

Shipping Costs: Who Pays? How Much?

Shipping costs can make or break a deal, so buyers need to know what your policies are.

Shipping big? Consider adding a freight-shipping calculator to your listing (see page 128).

You can charge a flat shipping fee or use eBay's shipping calculator, which determines shipping costs based on the winning bidder's address.

Comparison shop for shipping options and rates.

You can offer up to three shipping services. When you offer more than one, each service appears in your listing; if you use the shipping calculator, bidders can determine shipping charges for each service.

Tip: Offering multiple services is convenient for buyers, since it lets them choose which service they prefer based on where they live and how they like to receive packages. But it complicates your shipping routine. We typically offer just one service: US Postal Service for items under four pounds, and UPS or FedEx for anything heavier.

Should you insure? We say yes; see page 55.

You may need to charge sales tax to buyers in your home state. Consult your accountant, or check your local tax laws.

To remove a given service, click its Remove Service link. If you remove all services, you must either pay shipping costs yourself or require buyers to contact you for shipping costs—an extra step that could discourage bids.

Shipping Calculator

The shipping calculator is a handy way to give potential buyers an accurate assessment of their shipping fees. When you use it, your listing page contains a calculator that potential buyers can use to approximate shipping costs.

To use the shipping calculator, you'll need to have an idea of what your packaged item will weigh and the type of packaging you'll use.

For advice on many of these shipping details, see page 55.

More Payment and Shipping Details

We covered a lot of ground on the previous two pages, but we still have a bit more to go on eBay's Payment and Shipping Details page.

Specify Your Return Policy

Use this area to specify your return policy. For most items, we offer a 100-percent money-back guarantee. This gives potential bidders an extra measure of confidence, and our buyers rarely request refunds. (We're more cautious when it comes to returns on software and other media; see page 23.)

Return policy

☑ **Returns Accepted** - Specify a return policy. Learn More.

Item must be returned within 7 Days ▾

Refund will be given as Money Back ▾

Return Policy Details

> If you are unsatisfied with this item, for any reason, you have 7 days to return it for a full refund, including shipping. I will pay return shipping expenses.

341 characters left.

Spell Out Your Payment Instructions

The Payment Instructions box is another place to spell out your policies for payment, shipping, insurance, returns, and similar details. If you ship internationally, this is a good spot to let your potential buyers know how you ship and what you charge. The information you enter here appears on your listing page, in invoices that you send through eBay's Checkout system (opposite page), and in the end-of-auction notices that eBay sends to winning bidders.

Payment instructions

Give clear instructions to assist your buyer with payment and shipping.

Increase sales by offering a shipping discount in your description for multiple item purchases.

> Buyer to pay $3.85 for shipping/handling. Insurance is optional for an additional $1.30. Your item will be shipped via USPS Priority Mail. Please make your payment within 7 days of completion of the auction.
>
> If paying via PayPal, your shipping address MUST be confirmed. Your item will typically be shipped next business day after payment is received.

148 characters left.

Optional: Set Buyer Requirements

Review the buyer requirements you set in My eBay's Selling Preferences area (page 15). To change these preferences, click the Edit Preferences link.

Buyer requirements   Edit Preferences

Block buyers who:
✓ Have a feedback score of -1 or lower
✓ Have received 2 Unpaid Item strikes in the last 30 days

< Back | Continue >

Continue

When you've made your way to the bottom of the Payment and Shipping Details page, click the Continue button to move on. Then either skip to page 130 to wrap up your auction-creation adventure, or read on to learn about eBay's Checkout feature.

Express Checkout:
Setting Payment Preferences

With eBay's Checkout feature, you can streamline your invoicing and payment processes. If you're accepting PayPal payments, the Checkout feature is automatically turned on. If you aren't accepting PayPal, you can decide whether or not to use Checkout; as we describe here, there are pros and cons to doing so.

How Checkout works. When you use Checkout, your buyer will be able to pay you directly from the completed auction listing page—it will contain a Pay Now button and a summary of the payment methods you accept.

You won the item!

At the close of an auction, eBay automatically sends the high bidder an email containing the amount due and payment information. If you opt to use Checkout, this email also contains a link that takes the bidder to the checkout process.

You can also choose to assemble a pre-formatted invoice for your buyer. If you

sign in and go to the completed auction's listing page, you'll see a Send Invoice button.

Your item sold for US $36.50!
Buyer's email:
Buyer's Postal Code: 90740

Send Invoice >
To send your buyer payment information, click the **Send Invoice** button.

Click the button to go to the Send Invoice to Buyer page, where you'll find a pre-formatted invoice that you can customize with additional text and then send to your buyer (see page 110).

All of these post-sale timesavers are available to you when you activate the Checkout preference.

Should you Checkout? Many eBay sellers love the automation that Checkout provides, but on the downside, it takes the personal touch out of your transactions. We prefer to send invoices directly to buyers ourselves. Not only is this a bit more personal, but it can be more reliable, too—eBay's automatic invoices don't always go out right away. We'd rather do the emailing ourselves to insure proper contact with and satisfaction of our buyers.

Of course, using Checkout doesn't prohibit you from sending your own invoices. You might want to take advantage of the convenience of Checkout, but also follow up on your own with your buyers.

Setting Checkout Preferences

To set your Checkout preferences, go to the Preferences page in My eBay. Under Selling Preferences, click the Show link next to the Payment From Buyers heading (see page 15). Click the Edit link next to Use Checkout. You'll probably have to reenter your password to verify your identity, and then the Payment Preferences page appears.

To activate Checkout, check this box.   For PayPal pros and cons, see page 54.

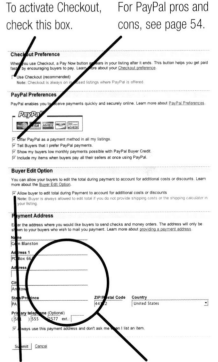

To permit buyers to alter shipping totals (for example, to incorporate a discount or extra shipping charge), check this box.

If you accept mailed payments, verify your address. This information appears in the invoices that eBay sends. **Note:** You don't need to supply your phone number.

Payment and Shipping Strategies

With all the payment and shipping options available to you, how do you decide which to accept and offer? Here's some advice.

Payment Options

As we noted on the previous pages, you can choose from several payment options. You might choose just one option, or you might choose several, depending on your willingness to accommodate buyers. Ultimately, the more forms of payment you accept, the more bidders you're likely to attract.

PayPal: Speed at a price

If you've done any buying on eBay, you're probably already familiar with PayPal. It's an online payment service that makes it easy to make and receive electronic payments using credit cards and other mechanisms.

From a seller's perspective, the great advantage of PayPal is immediacy: with most forms of PayPal payments, you receive your money instantly—no waiting for money orders to arrive in the mail, no waiting for checks to clear. A buyer clicks a few buttons, and the money is yours.

Or at least most of it is. PayPal takes a cut of your proceeds—generally, a few percentage points of the total amount.

Note: PayPal offers several types of accounts. In order to accept credit cards via PayPal, you must have a Premiere or Business account. For details, see www.paypal.com/accounts.

PayPal's immediacy has an obvious advantage for buyers, too: because you get paid sooner, they get their purchases sooner. If you accept PayPal, you're likely to attract more bidders. Indeed, by using the Advanced Search feature, eBay shoppers can even choose to search only those auctions that include PayPal as a payment option.

Tip: If you don't already have a PayPal account, you can still choose the PayPal option in the Payment & Shipping screen. Should your buyer choose to pay through PayPal, you can register for a PayPal account and be on your way.

Recommendation: For small-ticket auctions, you may find that PayPal's fees erode your profits too much, especially once you factor in eBay seller's fees. But for everything else, we heartily recommend PayPal. In the end, its fees are reasonable considering the tremendous convenience PayPal offers to buyers and sellers.

Other online payment services.

PayPal isn't the only game in town. You can opt to use one of the other online payment services, such as BidPay (www.bidpay.com). Each service has its own fees and policies. And keep in mind that although these services may some-times cost less than PayPal, they often lack the tight integration with eBay that PayPal offers. We'll see examples of this integration later.

Money order or cashier's check

Either of these options is like getting cash in the mail—but without the risk of theft, since the document is payable only to you. And there's nothing taken off the top, unlike a PayPal credit card payment.

On the downside, you lose some immediacy and convenience since you have to wait for the mail to bring your lucre and then you have to make a bank run to deposit it. More significantly, a money order or cashier's check is somewhat inconvenient for buyers, since they have to schlep to the bank or post office to get the document and they'll probably be asked to pay a small fee for it.

Warning: Counterfeit money orders are not unheard of. To help you recognize the real deal, the US Postal Service provides information at www.usps.com/postalinspectors/moalert.htm.

Recommendation: If you're willing to wait, by all means choose money order or cashier's check payment options. But think twice about making one of them your only payment option—that might discourage bidders.

Personal check

Buyers tend to like this option, but it can be inconvenient and risky for you as a seller. Before you can ship the item, you'll have to make a bank run to deposit your check and then wait a week or more until the check clears. (Never ship an item before a check has cleared.) And you risk the occasional bad check, which could cost you bank fees.

Recommendation: Yes, the most accommodating sellers will accept personal checks. But doing so means waiting longer for the auction to wrap up. We generally restrict our payment options to PayPal and money orders.

Shipping Options

Your choices here can affect your bottom line, as well as the convenience factor.

Who pays?

In our auctions, we almost always have buyers pay for shipping. Of course, you can elect to pay shipping costs yourself—and there's no question that the words "free shipping" in an item title and description have great appeal. But if you want to add this incentive to your auction, do the math and be sure your starting price or reserve price protect you from losing money on the auction.

Flat or variable shipping rates?

A flat shipping rate makes it easy for buyers to know what the total cost of your item will be. For small items, a flat shipping rate can make good sense.

If you're shipping large or heavy items, a flat rate is usually impractical, since shipping costs can vary significantly depending on your buyer's location. You'll probably want to use the eBay shipping or freight calculators that we described on the previous pages.

Packaging and handling fees

It takes time and effort to pack up a widget and drive it to your local shipping outlet, and you may have to pay for packing materials, too. Thus, it's entirely appropriate to incorporate a small handling fee when calculating your shipping price— maybe a dollar or so for most packages. Don't gouge your buyers, but don't neglect the fact that you're spending time and energy packing up their purchases.

Shipping insurance

We've said it before: we recommend insuring your shipments. In our experience, buyers don't balk at being required to buy insurance. If you're concerned about deterring some potential buyers, pay for the insurance yourself and mark up your shipping and handling fee a bit to cover the cost. And keep in mind that some shipping carriers include insurance up to a certain amount. United Parcel Service, for example, includes $100 worth of insurance with every package (see page 139).

Where will you ship? Will you ship to US buyers only? To the US and Canada? Or beyond? Going international can greatly increase your pool of potential buyers, but international shipping can be a lot more work, from filling out customs forms to converting currency, and more (page 130). If you're willing to ship internationally, be sure your payment instructions state that the buyer is responsible for any additional costs involved.

Review and Submit

You've worked your way through the many steps involved in creating an auction. Now's your chance to look at everything in one place, make any final changes, and get your auction started.

The Review & Submit page summarizes the details of your auction. See something you want to change? Click the appropriate link, and you'll return to the page where you can make the change.

This is your last chance to make sure everything is as it should be. You can edit a listing after an auction goes live, but there are some limitations to the kinds of changes you can make (see page 96). Bottom line: *Now* is the time to make sure your auction listing is accurate and complete.

The full Review & Submit page is quite long. We've divided it into six logical sections here to make it more manageable.

1. Backtrack If Necessary

At this stage, each of the previous pages is now a hyperlink; to jump back to a particular step, click its link.

2. Proofread Your Text

Title	Edit title
Handmade Ceramic Bowl Candy Dish, Ladybugs, Orange Pink	

Subtitle	Edit subtitle

Description	Edit description

This brightly colored, handmade bowl is both whimsical and useful.

The bowl is approximately 6" wide and stands 3" tall. The bowl is 2" deep at its center. The interior of the bowl is a bright orange, the exterior bright pink. The rim of the bowl is gold, the feet a bright red/orange.

Read and reread your title and item description. You don't want to sabotage your hard work with an overlooked typo. To make a change, click the link next to the title, subtitle, or description.

3. Check Your Photos

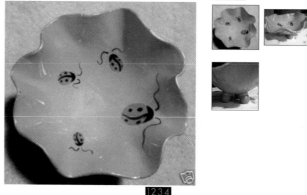

Edit Pictures

FREE Counters and Services from Andale

Gallery Picture(s)

NOTE: If your description or your pictures do not appear as expected, you may Edit your description or Edit your pictures to fix any problems.

Double-check that you've included the correct images. To change any images, use the Edit Your Pictures link.

4. Review the Details

Main Category	Edit Main Category
Home & Garden:Home Decor:Decorative Plates, Bowls:Ceramic, Porcelain (**#45479**)	

Second Category	Add second Category

Title & Description	Edit title & description
See above for preview of title, subtitle, Item Specifics and description.	

Pictures & Details	Edit pictures & details
Pictures:	3 picture(s) added to your listing. See above for preview of pictures
Duration:	7 days
Quantity:	1
Price:	**$9.95**
Buy It Now:	$24.95
Item Location:	Philo, California, United States
Listing Designer:	Theme: None Layout: Standard
Listing Upgrades:	Gallery
Free page counter:	Andale style See above for preview of counter

Payment & Shipping	Edit payment & shipping
Seller-accepted payment methods:	I accept PayPal. Payment will go to ▮▮▮▮▮▮▮▮ ▮▮▮; (Fees may apply if your buyer pays using PayPal) ; Other Payment Methods: Money order or Cashiers check;
Payment address:	▮▮▮▮▮▮ ▮▮▮▮ ▮▮▮ ▮▮▮, ▮▮ ▮▮▮▮▮ ▮▮▮ ▮▮▮▮
Buyer financing options:	Limited time offer! "Make no payments until 2006" will be displayed for items over $199 (**free** for sellers)
Ship-to locations:	Will ship to United States.
Shipping costs:	Charge flat shipping cost to my buyers

Shipping Cost	Services Available
$6.00	US Postal Service Priority Mail®
Shipping Insurance (required): $1.30	

When Will My Listing Appear?

Wondering how long it will take for your item to show up in the keyword and category searches? eBay updates its system periodically over the course of each day, so it may take a few hours for your listing to appear. However, your listing will show up almost immediately if buyers search by User ID.

This area details your category, pricing, and shipping information. It, too, provides links that you can use to revise any detail. Double-check all the specifics.

5. Note Your Fees

Step 2: Review the fees and submit your listing

Listing fees	
Insertion fee:	$ 0.35
Additional pictures:	0.30
Gallery:	0.35
Buy It Now Fee:	0.10
Total added listing fees:	**$ 1.10**

If your item sells, you will be charged a Final Value Fee. This fee is based on a percentage of the final sale price.

Current account balance before adding this item: **$18.23**

6. Make It So

< Back | **Submit Listing**

Your item will be listed on eBay and the above fees will be charged.

Review the fees and verify that you're being charged the appropriate amount. Perhaps you added additional features you didn't intend to. This is also a good chance to run the numbers, if you haven't yet. Remember, you'll be adding a final value fee to this total once you have a high bidder and your auction is complete.

When you're convinced everything is accurate, click Submit Listing. A congratulatory page will appear containing a link that will whisk you to your auction page. You'll also receive an email from eBay confirming your listing.

CHAPTER 3

The Pictures

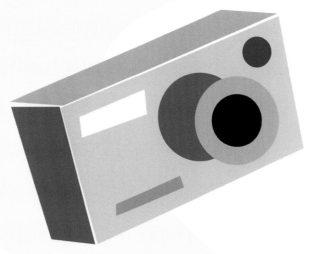

Pictures at a Glance

Just about any auction can use at least one picture. On the most obvious level, pictures enable potential buyers to see what you're selling. That may not be important if you're selling something whose appearance doesn't matter all that much—computer cables, for example. But it's critical for collectibles, clothes, artwork, furniture, and so much more. Your listing description may say, "Very cute poodle ashtray," but a photo will say it even better.

Pictures can also show flaws, wear and tear, and other traits that affect an item's value. The phrase "a few minor scratches" means one thing to Oscar Madison and quite another to Felix Unger. But a close-up photo of those scratches will tell the Odd Couple everything they need to know.

Finally, pictures have an important psychological benefit: they provide a measure of reassurance to potential bidders that your item really does exist. That reassurance can be important on eBay, where bidders are almost always buying from strangers.

Adding pictures to your listing is a fairly straightforward process. But *getting* the pictures is another matter. Should you take a digital photo? Or should you use a scanner? How many pictures should your listing have? And what should you do to show your item at its best?

We'll answer these questions and many more in this chapter. Let's start by looking at the big, well, picture.

Plan Your Shoot

Decide how many pictures you need to properly showcase your item, and determine the best way to acquire them (page 62).

Get the Pictures

Using a digital camera or a scanner, take the pictures. Light your item carefully, and compose your shots to show the item at its best.

Prepare the Pictures

Transfer the pictures to your computer. Perform any necessary fine-tuning, such as adjusting color balance or cropping out unwanted areas (page 74). Finally, resize the images for quick transfers over the Internet (page 78).

Upload Your Images

Using eBay Picture Services (page 44) or your own Web hosting service (page 43), transfer the images to make them available on your listing page.

Don't Steal Pictures

Some eBay sellers don't take pictures—they steal them. It's common to see professional product photography on listing pages for camera equipment, computers, electronic gear, music CDs, software, and more. Sellers find these photos on Web sites, save them on their hard drives, and upload them to their listing pages.

On one hand, it's easy to understand why folks pilfer images. If you're selling a Nikon 5700 digital camera, why not just grab that beautiful photo of it from the Nikon Web site? After all, it was taken by a professional photographer with

great equipment and a photo studio—it's got to look better than the one you'd take on your dining room table.

That may be true, but there are a few reasons why you shouldn't use those images. For starters, it's illegal. Those photos are protected by copyright law, and although Nikon is unlikely to slap a lawsuit on you, the fact is that you're using its imagery without its permission.

But more to the point, a stock product shot doesn't show *your* item. When you use someone else's photo, you lose some of the critical advantages that pic-

tures provide in the first place: they show *your* item's condition, and they reassure potential bidders that it really exists. A pilfered product shot does neither of these things.

A related issue deals with other eBay auctions. We've seen many instances of photos being lifted from another auction. This, too, is not kosher.

When we see an auction containing photos that have obviously been lifted from someone else's site—or someone else's auction—we think twice about bidding. So take your own photos, not someone else's. And if

you notice your photos appearing in other sellers' auctions, see page 73 for advice.

Note: There is one possible exception to this rule. In many eBay categories, including music CDs, video games, books, and movies, you have the option to use stock photography when creating your listing page (see page 39). You won't be violating any copyright laws when you use these stock images. For all the reasons we just outlined, however, we still recommend taking your own pictures, unless your item is brand new in its original packaging.

Planning Your Shoot

How you approach auction photography will depend on what you're selling. The number of photos you take, the way you take them, and even what equipment you use to take them can vary from one auction to the next.

To help you in your planning process, here's a roadmap to auction imaging.

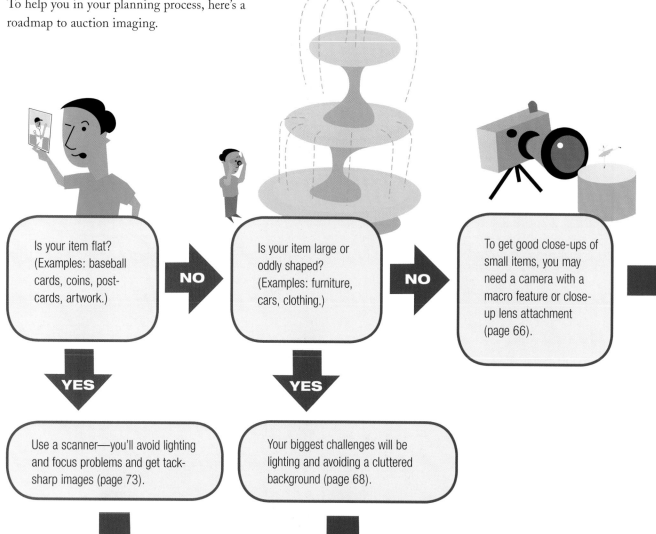

Is your item flat? (Examples: baseball cards, coins, postcards, artwork.)

NO

Is your item large or oddly shaped? (Examples: furniture, cars, clothing.)

NO

To get good close-ups of small items, you may need a camera with a macro feature or close-up lens attachment (page 66).

YES

Use a scanner—you'll avoid lighting and focus problems and get tack-sharp images (page 73).

YES

Your biggest challenges will be lighting and avoiding a cluttered background (page 68).

How many photos do you need in order to show the item? More photos let you show the item from a variety of angles as well as depict flaws or unique characteristics, but might increase your listing costs and can make your auction page slower to load.

Does your item move in an interesting or unique way? (Examples: cuckoo clock, kinetic sculpture, gull-wing Mercedes.)

Does your item have flaws or details that could benefit from a large photo?

Consider taking multiple shots of the item in various degrees of motion, then creating a picture slideshow for your listing (page 45).

Consider using the Supersize option, which displays large images (page 45).

Outfitting Your Photo Studio

We're big believers in doing things on the cheap, but we're also big believers in having the right tools for the job. To equip your auctions with the pictures they deserve, you're going to need some gear.

The good news is, digital imaging hardware and software have never been less expensive. And because eBay pictures need to be small in order to download quickly, you don't need to buy the latest, super-resolution, Hubble Space Telescope camera to take your shots. An older digital camera and scanner will do a fine job, and we know of a fabulous online auction site where you can find plenty of these devices.

And what about film? eBay's own photo tutorials list a third option for imaging: using a conventional camera and having your film processed by a lab that also scans and delivers your photos through the Internet or on a CD. This is an option in the same way that Morse code is an option for communicating: it works, but it's slow and antiquated. When you want to get an auction going, you probably don't want to wait several days—or even an hour or two—to get your photos developed. Although this option works, we recommend that you forgo film and go digital instead.

That said, let's go shopping.

Imaging Hardware

As we noted on the previous pages, whether you use a digital camera or a scanner will depend on what you're selling. Flat items—such as baseball cards and comics—are ideal subjects for a scanner, but for everything else, you'll need a camera.

Digital camera

The key specification to look at is resolution: how many pixels (dots) the camera uses to represent images. Resolution is measured in millions of pixels, or megapixels. A 2-megapixel camera will do a fine job for eBay work. Of course, it's easy to become addicted to digital photography and to start wanting to use your camera to produce large prints, too. In that case, look for a camera with a resolution of 4 megapixels or higher.

If you'll be taking close-ups of small items, you'll want to know how close you can get to an object while still being able to take a sharp photo. Look into the camera's minimum focus distance—it's often in the two-foot ballpark. Ideally, you want a camera with a macro mode—this lets you get much closer, typically within six inches or less, to your subject. Many cameras accept add-on macro lens attachments that let you get closer than the cameras' lenses normally permit.

Scanner

Again, resolution is the watchword, and with scanners, resolution is measured in dots per inch (dpi). And again, because Web photos have to be small, a cheap scanner will do a fine job for eBay work. Companies such as Epson and Canon now offer 1200-dpi scanners for under $50.

Optional: Lights and Tripod

If you plan to photograph items indoors, you may want to invest in some lights and a tripod. A tripod gives you a sturdy, stable place to mount your camera, and lights—well, you know what they do. For more advice on setting up a tabletop studio, see pages 66 and 71.

Imaging Software

We mean no disrespect to your skills as a photographer, but your photos will probably need some work. You may need to crop out unwanted portions of an image, such as the corner of the dining room table. You may want to fine-tune the color balance of an image taken indoors using room lighting. At the very least, you may need to downsize your images so that they transfer over the Internet quickly.

For these tasks, you'll need software. If you're running Microsoft Windows, a great choice is Adobe Photoshop Album. You can use it to import photos from a camera or scanner, store and manage a photo library, perform cropping, and downsize images for the Web. You can download a free "starter edition" of Photoshop Album from Adobe's Web site (www.adobe.com/ photoshopalbum). The starter edition does the job but has several features removed. The full version of Photoshop Album costs less than $50.

For the Apple Macintosh, we're huge fans of Apple's iPhoto, included with new Macs and available as part of Apple's iLife suite (www.apple.com/ilife). Like Photoshop Album, iPhoto handles everything from transferring photos, to managing them, to performing basic image editing. Note that iPhoto runs only on Apple's Mac OS X operating system. If you're running the older Mac OS 9.x, check out iView Multimedia's iView Media (www.iview-multimedia.com). It's inexpensive and has many of the same features found in iPhoto.

For more advanced image-editing tasks, we recommend Adobe Photoshop Elements. It costs less than $100 and is included with many digital cameras and scanners.

We show many of these programs in action later in this chapter.

EZcube: A Folding Photo Studio

If you'll be photographing small items, you may want to investigate the EZcube light tent. This clever fabric cube produces beautifully diffused light and provides a clean, uncluttered background—thus addressing two of the biggest challenges of online auction photography.

In the photo shown here, the EZcube is flanked by a pair of lights. But this light tent also delivers excellent results outdoors, even on the kind of sunny days that would normally cause glare and harsh shadows. Unfold the EZcube on your lawn, and you've got a portable photo studio.

The EZcube pictured here measures approximately 30 inches square and accommodates items up to 18 inches wide and 20 inches tall. Units in several other sizes are also available. You can buy them directly from the manufacturer (www.ezcube. com), who also sells them on eBay (search for *ezcube*).

Photographing Small Objects

People sell objects of all sizes on eBay, but much of what's for sale is smaller than a breadbox, if not a breadstick.

Photographing small objects can be tricky. Your photos need to show detail, especially any flaws that may affect the value of a collectible. Showing detail means getting close to your subject, and it's harder to keep items in focus when you're shooting close-ups.

Lighting is also more complicated at close range. When you're only a foot or so away from your subject, your camera's built-in flash will be too bright, and the photo will appear washed out. Turning off the flash will avoid a washed-out image, but may yield a dark or blurry photo unless you add extra lighting.

Some eBay sellers invest in special gear, such as a tripod and a set of lights and stands. We'd rather not spend the money and turn part of the house into a photo studio. The fact is, it isn't that hard to get a good-looking photo of a small object. You can get fine results by following a few simple rules. And if you sell small stuff all the time, you can turn a tabletop into a fine little photo studio.

Setting Up for Close-Ups

Although you can get good results by shooting outdoors with a hand-held camera, if you're going to be shooting close-ups all the time, you might find it more convenient to create a tabletop photo studio like the one shown here.

Lay some fabric or photographer's background paper atop the table, and drape the other end of it over a box or the back of a chair. Position your item on this background.

Hardware stores sell inexpensive work lights that you can clamp on to the back of a chair. Use two, positioning one on either side of your item at about a 45-degree angle.

A tabletop tripod is an inexpensive way to steady your camera. We've seen them on eBay for under $10.

Get Close

Most digital cameras have close-up, or macro, modes that enable you to get within a foot or even within inches of your subject. You can use a camera's macro mode to get up so close that even a tiny object will fill the frame.

 If your camera has a macro mode, it probably has a button with a tiny flower icon next to it. To switch to macro mode, press this button. To get as close as possible, put your camera's zoom lens in its maximum wide-angle position. Don't zoom in with macro mode turned on—you won't be able to get as close, and the images won't be as sharp.

Kill the Flash

If your camera has a built-in flash, it also has a button that lets you turn it off. The button is usually labeled with a lightning-bolt symbol. Press it until the camera's status display or LCD screen shows the "no flash" symbol. At close range, built-in flash is too bright.

With flash   Without flash

Use Bright, Diffused Light

We use a very bright light source all the time. It's a bit far away—about 93 million miles—but it's free and very reliable. It's the Sun.

But you have to know how to use this light source. Avoid photographing items in direct sunlight—you'll get a harshly lit photo with dark shadows that obscure detail.

Harsh light; cluttered background   Diffused light; clean background

A better approach is to shoot on a cloudy day or in the shade. Note that this can add a slightly bluish color cast to your photos. That won't be a problem for many items, but if color accuracy is important for your item, switch your camera's white-balance setting to "cloudy." See your camera's manual for specific instructions.

If you don't want to futz with your camera's white-balance settings, just take the photo. If its color is way off, you can always adjust it later (see page 75).

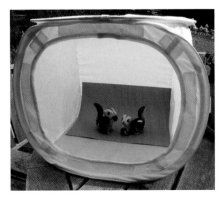

The EZcube light tents mentioned on page 65 are ideal for small objects. The salt and pepper shakers above were photographed in the smallest EZcube model, the 12-inch square Micro. To avoid a bright white background, we put a sheet of colored paper beneath the items (left).

Photographing Big Items

Looking to unload that walk-in humidor or those old poodle skirts? First things first: please don't tell our spouses. They'll bid.

With that out of the way, let's look at the special considerations behind photographing big and unusually shaped items.

For large items, your primary challenges are background and lighting. You may not be able to set up a plain backdrop behind a big item, so you'll need to take steps to avoid a cluttered background that detracts from your item.

As for lighting, those clamp-on work lights that we recommended on page 66 may not be enough to illuminate a large item. You may have to shoot outdoors or resort to using your camera's built-in flash. If your eBay selling career will lean toward the large, you may want to invest in some larger lights.

Then there's "oddly shaped" items, the biggest category of which is clothing. Unless you can figure out a way to prop a pair of pants against a wall for a photo shoot, you'll have to take some special steps to make clothing look its best. We've provided some tips on page 71.

Background Check

A cluttered background draws attention away from a subject. If your item is light enough to move, consider positioning it against a plain wall or fence. As an alternative, try to drape a sheet or some photographer's background paper behind and beneath the item.

For very large or heavy items, these techniques may not be practical. In that case, compose your photo to avoid the worst of the clutter, as shown in these shots of a 400-pound ceramic mosaic bench by artist Jan Hinson. We weren't about to move the bench, but by simply changing our camera position, we were able to omit the worst parts of the background and get a better shot.

Cluttered

Uncluttered

This illustrates a key tip that applies to all your photographic endeavors: study the background before you shoot. Our minds are great editors—we subconsciously ignore background clutter. But a camera sees all, so before you snap that shutter, look at the entire frame and adjust your position to get rid of that telephone pole, neighbor's house, or other visual noisemaker.

Shoot at an Angle

While we're talking composition, here's a related tip that applies to items of all sizes: don't shoot straight-on. That's a sure-fire way to give an item a flat, two-dimensional appearance.

Instead, shoot items at an angle. This lets people see the side of the item and yields a more attractive photo.

In this example, we've also draped a sheet behind and beneath the rocking chair to avoid a cluttered background.

If all sides of your item are interesting, take multiple shots and consider buying the Picture Show slide show upgrade (page 45).

Straight-on

At an angle

Shed Some Light

Until the folks at EZcube come out with a room-sized cube, you'll need to work a little harder to light large items. One option is to shoot them outdoors, preferably in the shade or on a cloudy day. If that isn't an option, you have a few alternatives.

Shoot near a window. Get as much natural light as you can.

Add lights. Four-foot fluorescent work lights are bright and inexpensive. To avoid ugly green color casts, be sure to change your camera's white-balance mode to fluorescent (see page 72).

Boost your ISO speed. Many digital cameras have controls that let you increase their ISO speed, essentially improving their light sensitivity. Without getting into technical details, changing your ISO speed to 200 or 400 can often help you get better shots in low light.

Use the flash (cringe). We've made no secret of our dislike for built-in flash. But if it's all you have, use it. Just be sure to photograph your item at an angle so you don't get bright glare spots.

Don't Forget the Close-Ups

Big items often have small details that are important to potential buyers. Maybe they're flaws, such as scratches or stains. Or maybe they're desirable details, such as an obscure manufacturer's nameplate. In either case, take sharp close-ups to give your bidders the details they need.

If you need to get extremely close, use your camera's macro feature, as described on page 66.

Picture Tips

Indoor Strategies

If a blizzard or a nosy neighbor prevents you from shooting outside, move indoors—to a kitchen or dining-room table, or to a card table set up in front of a bright window. (Keep that flash turned off.)

If you don't have enough light, your camera will use a slow shutter speed (a longer exposure time). Unless you have the steady hands of a neurosurgeon, your photo will probably be blurry.

One solution is to use a tripod. A cheaper solution is to throw more light on the subject with a desk lamp or a set of hardware store work lamps clamped on to a couple of chairs. Position the lights as shown on page 66. Avoid bright light behind the item—*backlighting*, as it's called, may flatter a model's hair, but yields bad eBay pictures.

If you're adding supplemental lighting, your photos may have a yellowish color cast. If that's bothersome, switch your camera's white-balance setting to "tungsten."

Look at the LCD

On most cameras, the viewfinder doesn't show exactly what the lens is seeing. That isn't a problem when you're shooting a beach scene, but when you're shooting close-ups, you may risk cutting off part of your subject. To avoid this, compose your shot while looking at the camera's LCD screen, which does show exactly what the lens sees. But note that holding the camera at arm's length can increase the chances of a blurry photo; here's where a tripod really helps.

Show the Items in a Set

If the item you're selling is comprised of multiple pieces or components, consider taking a *group shot*—a picture showing the pieces that come with the item.

eBay shoppers can't open up a box and paw through its contents, but a group shot is the next best thing. It enables shoppers to see what's included with your item, and it proves that you have all the pieces.

If one of the items is the star of the show, consider taking a separate close-up photo of it.

Choose a Contrasting Background

Don't just set an item on a tabletop or driveway and fire away. Create a background for it—solid-colored cloth, colored construction paper, a bed sheet, or the seamless background paper that photographers use.

Whatever background material you use, choose something with a color that contrasts with the item. Don't photograph a silver pin against a white background—it will look bland. There's a reason jewelers display their wares against dark velvet: the contrast makes the jewelry look brighter.

How Big is It?

It's hard to judge an object's size when there's nothing else in the photo. That isn't a problem for small items with an obvious size—for example, a Hot Wheels car or a fountain pen.

But for jewelry and other items whose size can vary hugely, you might consider including something a bidder can use as a visual reference—a ruler or a quarter, for example.

The Low-Budget Countertop Studio

Here's a kitchen-countertop setup that we often use for photographing small and medium-sized items.

Our background: a sheet of paper yanked from a printer and taped to the countertop. Our lighting: the kitchen lights. The tabletop tripod keeps the camera steady, enabling us to turn off the flash.

Our background (the sheet of printer paper) is too small to completely fill the frame, so we crop our photos as shown on page 74.

Softwear: Clothing Considerations

Spend a few minutes browsing eBay's clothing categories, and you'll quickly see some examples of how *not* to photograph clothes. A sweater draped across a plaid chair? Not good. A shirt stretched across a paunchy guy's torso? Worse.

Mail-order catalogs spend a lot of money making clothes look their very best, and that includes hiring models that have had more body work than a 1972 Pinto. You don't have to go to these extremes to make clothes look appealing.

Let them drape. We've seen a lot of clothing listings where garments are laid out on a sheet or wall-to-wall carpeting, and then photographed. These sellers have the right idea—keep the background uncluttered. The problem is, clothing doesn't drape properly when it's pressed flat against the floor. Clothes appear more natural when they're, well, vertical.

Mannequins versus hangers. Many eBay sellers recommend buying a mannequin to model clothing. That's good advice,

and we've seen mannequins on eBay for about $20. But for sweaters and shirts, a hanger also works fine. Show some class and use a wooden one.

Color concerns. Accurate color is important in clothing photography. If you're shooting indoors under room lighting, be sure to adjust your digital camera's white-balance setting to avoid a yellow or green color cast.

Tag sale. If you're selling a new garment that still has its tags, show the tags in at least one of the photos.

Heel! If you're selling shoes, take several photos from different angles so potential bidders can see the big picture. Ditto for hats and other accessories.

Don't forget the text. Good pictures don't eliminate the need to also include complete details, including sizes and measurements, in your item description. Given that sizing has become less meaningful, particularly with women's clothing, it's essential to include key measurements, such as waist, arms, and inseam.

More Picture Tips

What is White Balance?

We recommend adjusting your camera's white balance setting to avoid color casts when shooting under artificial lighting. Here's why.

Few light sources are pure white; they have a color cast of some kind. Incandescent lamps (light bulbs) cast a yellowish light, while fluorescent light is greenish. Even outdoors, there can be variations—bluish in the morning, reddish in the evening. Each of these light sources has a different color temperature.

Our eyes and brains compensate for this. Digital cameras try to do so with a feature called *automatic white balance,* but they aren't as good at it as we humans. That's why many cameras have manual white balance adjustments that essentially let you tell the camera, "Hey, I'm shooting under incandescent (or fluorescent) lights now, so make some adjustments in the way you record color."

White balance adjustments are usually labeled WB, and are labeled with icons representing cloudy skies ☁, incandescent lamps ☀, and fluorescent lighting ☲. You'll probably have to switch to your camera's manual-exposure mode to access its white balance settings.

In the examples below, the background is a white sheet of paper, and the light source is a fluorescent tube (to be honest, a kitchen range light). The upper image has a greenish cast; in the lower image, we've changed the white balance to fluorescent.

Without correct white balance

With correct white balance

Is fiddling with the white balance worth the trouble? It depends on what you're selling. For clothing, art, fabric, and other items where color is critical, it won't hurt to experiment with various white balance settings.

Picture Theft

To discourage unscrupulous sellers from boosting your pictures, consider adding a *watermark* to them. This is a piece of text—anything you like—that is faintly imprinted on a picture. Put your User ID on your auction pictures, and they're a lot less likely to get boosted.

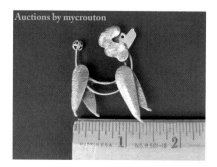

You can use Photoshop Elements to add a watermark. Create a text layer, type your text, and then lower its opacity to about 50 percent or so. Save the results as a JPEG file, following the guidelines on page 78.

You might find it easier to use a watermarking utility. We're fond of two: DropWaterMark from LAJ Design (www.lajdesignsw.com; available for Windows and Mac, $16.50) and ImageWell (www.xtralean.com; Mac only, free).

eBay's extra-cost Picture Manager subscription service (page 43) also provides a watermarking option.

And what if you find that another seller is reusing your photos? We say report the bum—go to www.ebay.com/help/confidence/vero-image-text-theft.html.

Avoiding Reflections

If you're selling highly reflective items, such as metal teapots and mirrors, you can avoid shooting self-portraits by positioning your camera at an angle instead of photographing the item straight-on. Another option is to use an EZcube light tent, which includes a door containing a narrow slit for your camera's lens.

Replacing Self-Hosted Photos

As described on page 96, eBay doesn't allow you to add or remove photos on auctions that have already received bids. However, if you're hosting your own images (see page 43), you can work around this prohibition: simply replace one or more of the auction's existing photos with new ones, while keeping the pictures' filenames the same.

For example, let's say you're selling a table lamp, and your auction has one photo named lamp.jpg. As the auction progresses, you begin to wish your photo had done a better job of showing the Leonard Nimoy figurine at the top of the lampshade. Simply take a better photo, name it lamp.jpg, and replace the original one on your server.

Scanning Tips

Using a scanner instead of a camera? Here are a few tips for better scans.

Clean the glass. Use glass cleaner and heavy-duty paper towels, such as Viva, to clean the glass before you scan.

Get the resolution right. eBay pictures are small, so you don't have to scan at high resolution. 75 to 100 dots per inch (dpi) will deliver fine results. If you want to focus in on part of an item—for example, to get a close-up of a damaged envelope—scan at 200 or 300 dpi, and then crop the resulting scan as described on page 74.

We admit it: figuring out the correct relationship between scanning resolution and image size can be a brain-bending exercise. Fortunately, most scanning software provides presets for common scanning scenarios, such as scanning for the Web or for color inkjet output. Use the "Web" setting if your software has one, and you'll usually get fine results for eBay.

Preview, crop, then scan. Chances are the item you're scanning is smaller than your scanner's bed. Rather than scan the entire bed, do a preview scan first. Next, use your scanner software to draw a

crop rectangle around the item you want to scan. Now do the final scan.

And if your item is bigger than the scanner bed? Either shoot it using a camera, scan it in sections and then assemble

the sections in an image-editing program, or simply do what some eBayers do: add a disclaimer to your item description to the effect that the picture doesn't show the entire item because it didn't fit on your scanner.

Try descreening. If you're scanning photos that were printed on a press—baseball cards, old magazine ads, and the like—try using your scanning software's descreening function. It smoothes out the dot patterns that are used to print photos. If the results look a little soft, try again with descreening off.

Refining Your Pictures

Good lighting, sharp focus, and an uncluttered background will get you 90 percent of
the way toward a great eBay picture. Now it's
time for the last 10 percent.

You may want to refine your shots by cropping
out unwanted stuff, such as the tabletop that
appears on either side of your background.
If the image looks a bit dull or washed out,
you may want to lighten or darken it.

Today's digital imaging programs have
automatic features that can perform some of
these steps for you with a single mouse click.
We'll cover those auto-fixers here; on the
following pages, we'll look at some manual
options that give you more control. Many of
our instructions are for Adobe Photoshop,
Photoshop Elements, and Photoshop Album,
but the underlying concepts apply to other
imaging programs, too.

If you use eBay Enhanced Picture Services
(introduced on page 42), you can also perform
some basic photo refinements right within
your browser. As the sidebar on the opposite
page describes, eBay Enhanced Picture
Services lets you crop photos as well as tweak
their brightness and contrast.

But eBay Enhanced Picture Services is no
digital darkroom, and it runs only with the
Internet Explorer browser on Microsoft
Windows systems. For these reasons,
we recommend using a dedicated imaging
program for photo fine-tuning.

Cropping

For these examples, we photographed a Hall China creamer using
the countertop setup shown on page 71.

Using your imaging program's Crop tool , crop the photo to focus
in on your subject and remove unwanted parts of the background.
Here's how it looks in Adobe's free Photoshop Album Starter Edition.

Step 1: Activate the Crop
tool by clicking it.

To do the deed, click Apply.
(In Photoshop, press the Return
or Enter key. In iPhoto, click the
Crop button.)

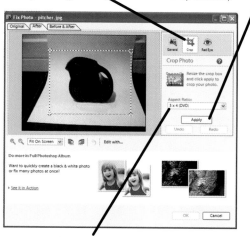

Step 2: eBay pictures are rect-
angular, with a 4:3 aspect
ratio—four units of width for
every three units of height. To
ensure your cropped picture will
have these proportions, constrain the cropping rectangle
(see the tip below).

Drag within the image to draw
the cropping rectangle.
Anything outside this rectangle
will be removed. To fine-tune
the rectangle's size, drag its
corners. To move the rectangle,
drag within it.

Constraining crops. To constrain a crop area in Photoshop Album,
choose 3 x 4 (DVD). In Photoshop and Photoshop Elements, click
the Front Image button in the toolbar after you activate the Crop tool
and before you begin drawing the crop rectangle. In Apple's iPhoto,
choose 4 x 3 (Book) from the Constrain pop-up menu.

Adjust Color and Levels

This is an optional step, but it's often worth the effort. By fine-tuning color and exposure (technically, *tonality*), you can fix a photo that's too light or too dark.

The one-click way. Most imaging programs have one-click fix features for adjusting color, tonality, and contrast.

In Photoshop Album's General Fixes window, use the Auto Color, Auto Levels, and Auto Contrast buttons. In Photoshop Elements, choose Auto Smart Fix from the Enhance menu, or click the Quick Fix button near the upper-right corner of the Photoshop Elements window to display the Quick Fix controls shown here. In Apple's iPhoto, use the Enhance button in iPhoto's Edit mode.

Here's our creamer photo before and after applying some fixes using Photoshop Elements' Quick Fix window.

Tip: You may not have to use all of your program's auto-fix features. If your software has an auto-levels feature, start there; it alone may give your picture the punch it needs.

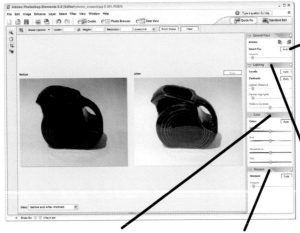

To refine the photo's brightness and color balance with one click, click the Auto button in the Smart Fix area. Or fine-tune the smart fix by dragging the Amount slider.

Use the controls in the Lighting palette to adjust shadows and highlights.

If your photo has an unwanted color cast, the adjustments in the Color palette can help.

A little bit of sharpening can add crispness, but don't overdo it, lest the photo look artificial.

Refining Pictures the eBay Way

If you use the Internet Explorer browser and Microsoft Windows, you can use eBay Enhanced Picture Services to crop photos and adjust their brightness and contrast.

Rotate 90 degrees.

Crop tool: select it, then drag the blue corners shown here to indicate which portion of the photo you want to keep.

Automatically adjusts brightness and contrast.

Displays a separate window containing additional buttons for adjusting brightness and contrast.

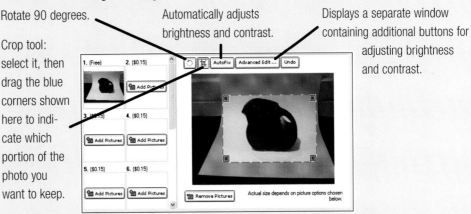

Extra Credit: Advanced Picture Polishing

Chances are the techniques we described on the previous pages will be all you need to make your pictures sparkle. But if you're about to auction a particularly valuable item, you might want to bypass your software's auto-fix features and use its manual controls to modify tonal levels and color balance.

You might even want to put on your digital retoucher's hat and alter the image itself—for example, to digitally remove the edge of a desk. You should never retouch the item you're selling—digitally removing a crack in a ceramic pitcher is unethical and down-right deceptive—but there's nothing wrong with retouching the background to make your item look its best.

You certainly don't have to sweat these details for every eBay picture you take. But for those special items—and for your non-eBay pictures—these techniques can dramatically improve your shots.

Adjusting Tonality By Hand

For more control, dive into your software's level controls to modify tonal levels. In Photoshop, press Control-L (Windows) or ⌘-L (Mac) to display the Levels dialog box. Use the Levels controls as shown here in Photoshop Elements. (In Apple's iPhoto, use the Levels controls in the Adjust panel.)

This graph, called a *histogram*, shows the distribution of pixels in the image, from black on the far left to white on the far right. Here, the graph is showing a lack of white information in the image—notice there's no data near the right edge of the histogram.

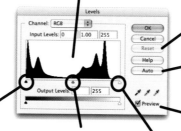

Click Reset to restore the original levels.

To have Photoshop Elements automatically adjust the levels, click Auto.

To get a quick before-and-after view of your changes, uncheck and then recheck Preview.

To adjust highlights and other bright areas, drag the white point slider to the left.

To adjust shadows and other dark areas, drag the black point slider to the right.

To adjust the mid-tones of the image, drag this slider. To brighten the image, drag to the left.

To improve the picture of our creamer, we moved the white point slider to the left so that it's beneath where the white data in the image begins. We also moved the mid-tone slider to the left to brighten things up. Quick tweaks like these are often all it takes to improve a picture.

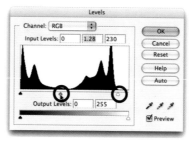

Retouching with the Clone Stamp Tool

For removing unwanted parts of an image, it's hard to beat the clone stamp tool provided by Photoshop, Photoshop Elements, and many other imaging programs.

The clone stamp tool lets you copy one part of an image to another part—to essentially paint on one area using pixels from another area.

When we shot this photo of a salt-and-pepper shaker, we accidentally shot a mouse cable and the edge of the desk, too. Using the clone stamp tool, you can paint problems like these away.

Before

After

First, click the clone stamp tool ![icon] in the tools palette. Next, press the Alt key (Option on the Mac) and then click near the area where you want to paint. This sets the *source point*—the area from which Photoshop will pick up pixels as you paint.

Next, paint over the unwanted area by dragging across it. As you do, Photoshop picks up pixels from the source point and deposits them where you're painting.

Photoshop is picking up pixels from here... ...and depositing them here.

Work carefully, using different brush sizes if necessary. Once you get the hang of it, you'll be fixing photos and making mischief (try giving your friend a third eyeball).

Preparing Pictures for the Internet

Digital picture files tend to be big—too big to transfer over the Internet quickly, even with speedy connections.

Because of this, the last step before putting a picture on a Web site (or emailing it to someone) is to put the picture on a diet: to make its dimensions smaller and perform some other steps that make the picture more compact and faster to transfer.

This process also applies to eBay pictures, with one big exception: If you use eBay Enhanced Picture Services (introduced on page 42), you're spared this chore. eBay Enhanced Picture Services automatically makes your images smaller.

As you may recall, the first time you use Enhanced Picture Services, a small software program installs on your computer. This program not only gives you the image-tweaking controls we've described previously, it also does the downsizing for you *before* uploading your pictures to eBay. It's a big convenience that eliminates an often-confusing part of the picture-preparation process.

But as we said earlier, Enhanced Picture Services works only on Microsoft Windows machines running Internet Explorer. You may be among the millions of people who use Macs or other browsers, such as Firefox. Or maybe you're planning to host your own pictures rather than have eBay do it.

If you're in these groups, you have a couple of extra steps to perform before uploading your pictures.

The Importance of Good Dieting

How important is this digital dieting stuff? It's critical. If you don't use eBay Enhanced Picture Services and you simply try to upload a four-megapixel photo to eBay, you'll get an error message. That's because eBay limits the size of a photo to roughly 600K—smaller than a typical two-megapixel photo.

Thus, if you're going to use eBay to dish out your auction photos, you have two choices. You can use eBay Enhanced Picture Services, whose little browser-based program resizes photos for you before uploading. Or you can perform the steps we've outlined here to downsize photos yourself before uploading.

Digital Dieting Explained

Preparing an image for eBay involves making its dimensions smaller and specifying compression settings.

Let's get small. We've already mentioned that eBay prefers pictures with dimensions that are 400 pixels wide by 300 pixels tall. Chances are you're starting with original images that are much larger. For example, a two-megapixel camera takes pictures that are 1600 pixels wide by 1200 pixels tall. Your first step when preparing images will be to make their dimensions smaller.

Let's get fuzzy. Although eBay can accept several kinds of image formats, it's best to use the JPEG format. The JPEG format shrinks files by discarding image information, a process called *lossy compression*. In essence, JPEG compression makes picture files smaller by making the pictures look somewhat crummy. Just how crummy is up to you—you can dial in how much compression to apply when you're preparing a picture. More compression means a faster-loading—but fuzzier—picture.

(And by the way, virtually all digital cameras use the JPEG format, but cameras compress images very lightly in order to retain image quality.)

To recap, preparing an image for the Internet is a two-step process. First, make the image's pixel dimensions smaller, then adjust compression settings before you save.

Preparing Pictures with Photoshop

The Save for Web command in Photoshop and Photoshop Elements makes it easy to prepare pictures.

If you've done any retouching or refining, save the original version of your picture before performing the following steps. That way, you'll always have its original, high-resolution version.

Then, choose Save for Web from the File menu. The Save for Web dialog box appears.

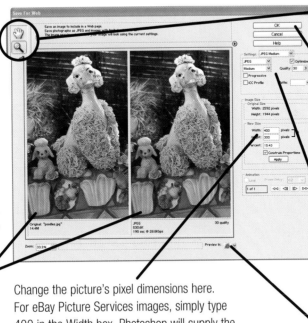

Before-and-after views show the results of your compression settings.
Tip: Change the picture's dimensions first, then adjust compression settings while looking at the preview.

Change the picture's pixel dimensions here. For eBay Picture Services images, simply type 400 in the Width box. Photoshop will supply the Height value for you as long as the Constrain Proportions box is checked. To downsize the picture, click Apply.

Use the Hand tool to scroll the image previews, and the Zoom tool to zoom in and out.

When you're ready to save the small image, click OK. Use a different name for the image to avoid replacing the original.
Tip: If you're preparing several pictures for one auction, make them easy to find by stashing them all in one folder.

Specify JPEG compression settings here. Photoshop provides several presets—JPEG Medium is a fine place to start. If you want to fine-tune settings, use the Quality control.

To preview how your image will look in a browser, click this icon.

Special Sizing Considerations

Tall or wide photos. Let's say your picture doesn't have the 4:3 proportions that we recommend—maybe you cropped without constraining your imaging software's crop tool—but you're still planning to use eBay Picture Services to host it. In this case, you should downsize the picture so that its longest dimension matches eBay's requirement for that dimension.

For example, if your original picture is very wide, specify a width of 400 pixels and let your software calculate the correct height. For a very tall picture, specify a height of 300 pixels and let your software come up with the right width.

Your own Web hosting. Hosting your own pictures? You can make their dimensions anything you like. But remember, bigger pictures mean longer downloads. Think twice about using a picture larger than 800 pixels wide by 600 tall. In fact, you should generally aim much lower—in the 400 by 300 ballpark.

Tip: When resizing images that you'll be hosting, jot down their width and height pixel values.

You can use these values in the HTML <img> tag as described on page 89.

Supersizing. If you're buying the Supersize picture upgrade (described on page 45), your pictures should be at least 440 pixels wide by 330 pixels tall. The maximum size is 800 by 600 pixels.

CHAPTER 4

Text and Formatting: The Look of the Page

Words that Sell: The Process of Text

An old saying goes, "A picture is worth a thousand words, but it takes words to say that." A newer saying goes, "Pictures are optional on eBay auctions, but words aren't."

You get the idea: Pictures are important, but it's the text you write that enables other eBayers to find your auction and inspires them to bid.

Where text is concerned, you have a few jobs, each different from the others. First assignment: the item title. Write a phrase that snares people who are using eBay's search feature to locate items like yours, and do it in 55 characters or less.

Next assignment: describe your item, including specifics such as size, color, condition, year of manufacture, number of appendages—whatever facts and figures apply to what you're selling.

As you write your item description, you might also perform a third job: formatting it. By using eBay's HTML editor or pecking in codes by hand, you can make text bold, change its color and typeface, create new paragraphs, and more. (But not *too* much more—you will see that we discourage creating fancy listing layouts or using hokey listing design templates.)

Pages 38 and 39 describe the mechanics of creating an item title, optional subtitle, and description. In this chapter, we examine the art of eBay writing: what to say, what not to say, and how to make what you say look good.

What Makes Good eBay Writing?

An eBay listing isn't literature, nor is it a glossy advertisement. It's a unique blend of classified ad, brochure, personal home page, and legal proposal. By their contents and appearance, many listings will tell you things about the people who created them. This is one of the charms of eBay—instead of page after page of snazzy copywriter's prose, every page has a different voice.

At the same time, every listing should also have four things.

Honesty. eBay's existence depends on it, and it all starts with the listing: a title that isn't misleading and a description that includes full disclosure about an item's age, condition, flaws, and missing parts.

Thoroughness. The more you tell people about your item, the more likely they'll bid and the less likely they'll email you with questions. Write your descriptions as if there aren't accompanying pictures. You don't have to write a book, but you should give people enough information to make a bidding decision. And that includes details about your shipping and payment policies.

Readability. Rainbow-colored headings, animated bunnies, waving flags—keep them off your listings. Why add graphics that are going to distract people from your text? You want your description to be as easy to read as possible. That also means avoiding ALL CAPITAL letters. Learn to love your Shift key.

Individuality. We hate auctions that contain nothing but cut-and-pasted marketing text from a manufacturer's Web site. Use your own words. Tell us about *your particular* item. If you want us to read the manufacturer's hype, put a link to it in your description (see page 88). And needless to say, don't cut and paste text from another eBayer's auction.

The Nuts and Bolts of Text

You can type your item description directly into the text box on the Describe Your Item page, but we don't recommend doing so. Web browsers make lousy word processors—their editing features are limited, and they don't let you save your work as you write. Here's a better way to work.

Step 1. Process words.

Use a word processor to write your item descriptions. Don't do any fancy formatting here—your Web browser won't recognize it. (You can type HTML formatting codes, though, as we describe on page 86.) Check your spelling, and save your work as you go. You'll be protected from a computer crash, and you'll have your original text to reuse or adapt for future auctions.

Step 2. Copy your text.

When you're description is just so, save it. Next, choose Select All from the Edit menu, then choose Copy from the Edit menu.

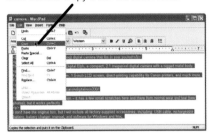

Step 3. Paste into your browser.

When you get to the Describe Your Item page, click in the Item Description box and choose Paste from the Edit menu. If you're using eBay's HTML editor, format your text as desired (see page 39).

Remember that you can preview how your final description will look by clicking Preview Description.

Save Time: Store Your Boilerplate Text

You may have some standard text that you frequently use in your item descriptions. Maybe it's a phrase describing a type of item you sell all the time. Or maybe it's a reminder of your payment policies.

To avoid repetitive typing (and typos), stash this text in a word processor file. When you need the text, open the file, copy the text, and then paste it into your item description.

Using inserts. If you use Microsoft Windows and the

Internet Explorer browser, you have another option: create what eBay calls *inserts*.

Inserts are tidbits of boilerplate text; an insert can contain up to 1,000 characters, including HTML code. Inserts are stored on eBay's servers, so you can access them from any Windows computer running Internet Explorer. That's handy when you're traveling and can't wait to get home to post that Tom Cruise bobble head you found in a thrift shop.

To create, edit, and use inserts, use the Inserts menu in the enhanced description editor.

Creating a new insert involves typing the text you want to store as well as a name for the insert; the name appears in the Inserts menu, as shown here.

Here, we've created one insert listing our payment policies and another containing a phrase that tells bidders an item ships in its original box with all manuals and accessories.

These eBay-created inserts let you easily direct bidders to your other auctions and encourages them to add you to their favorites list.

Tips for Text

Titling Tips

How should you use those precious 55 characters? Answer: very carefully. Here are some good and not-so-good examples.

Good Titles

Think like a searcher. What other terms might lead people to your item? Just be sure they apply to your item—see "Don't keyword spam," below.

Bad Titles

Insufficient data. The name of the movie is *The Matrix,* and this title won't show up in searches for that phrase.

EASY RIDER, 8 Lobby Cards, Mint, Peter Fonda

W@W!!!! SUPER Matrix photos, Keenu Reeves

Start at the top. Begin the title with the term you think shoppers are most likely to be interested in.

Give the facts. Spell out what it is you're selling. These examples would also snag people searching for *lobby cards* and *MP3 music player.*

Don't waste space. No one ever searches for *W@W!!* or other hype terms or punctuation characters. So why use them? If you want to set your title apart, buy the bold upgrade (see page 47) or consider a subtitle (see the sidebar on the opposite page).

Spelling is everything. Be sure to spell names and other critical keywords accurately.

Avoid all capital letters. It's okay to use all caps occasionally (for example, MINT), but they're hard to read—don't use them for an entire title.

NEW Apple iPod 40GB MP3 music player with dock, NIB, NR

PANASONIC TV, SIMILAR TO SONY TRINITRON

Be specific. If any key specifications may set your item apart, include them. Make it easy for searchers to see how your item differs from others.

Sweeten the deal. Add details that might further entice a shopper. See Appendix B for a list of common auction abbreviations and their definitions. If you have room, consider using any abbreviations appropriate to your item.

Don't keyword spam. Using words unrelated to your item in order to snag searchers is called *keyword spamming.* Technically, it's trademark infringement. More to the point, it's against eBay rules and could get your auction cancelled.

Description Tips

Know your subject. We're instantly turned off by descriptions that contain phrases like, *I got this widgetator at a pawn shop. I don't really know anything about widgetators, but this one hums when you plug it in, so it must work.* If you're selling it, you should know something about it. Vague descriptions yield disappointing results.

Be specific. How fast or big or heavy is it? What color or size is it? Do you have the original box? Manual? Accessories?

Do some Web searches for your item; if you find some interesting pages, include their addresses in your description. For collectibles, consider using any official grading definitions (mint, fair, and so on) that apply. Be sure to use these terms properly; see Appendix C.

Be yourself. Is there a funny anecdote behind your item? Say so: *I found this inflatable Spiro Agnew swimming pool toy in my parents' attic, and couldn't wait to put it on eBay.* Don't be afraid to inject a little personality into your description.

Practice full disclosure. If you're selling a multi-piece item and some pieces are missing, say so: *The shoe and the Get Out of Jail Free cards are missing.* Describe any scratches or other flaws in detail. If you show the flaws in your pictures, say so: *The guitar has a four-inch gash in its side (see photo).*

Make it readable. Text on a computer screen is difficult to read. To improve readability, use paragraph breaks, starting a new paragraph every couple of sentences or so. If the description has a list of features, consider formatting them as a bulleted list (see page 87). And never write a description in all-capital letters.

Encourage questions. Offer to answer any questions potential bidders may have.

Promote yourself. If you have other auctions going on, say so near the bottom of your description: *This is just one of the I Dream of Jeannie collectibles that I am selling, so please check out my other auctions.*

Go easy on the fine print. It's a good idea to summarize your payment and shipping policies at the end of your item description. However, we see many auctions whose descriptions end with paragraphs of threatening text: *We will report non-paying bidders and leave negative feedback. Your winning bid is a legally binding contract. Winning bidder must pay within ten days or we will retaliate.* The warnings go on and on.

We know how frustrating it is to be burned by deadbeat bidders, but remember, they're the minority. Classy stores don't have *We prosecute shoplifters* signs everywhere you turn, and your listings shouldn't have the equivalent.

If you do have very complicated payment or shipping policies—or you insist on warning your customers instead of welcoming them—here's a compromise. Create an About Me page (see page 150) that lists your policies (and your threats, if you must), and then say something like, *Note: My shipping and payment policies are very strict. Please see my About Me page for details.*

Now Showing with Subtitles

For 50 cents, you get an additional opportunity to reel in searchers by adding another 55 characters of text that appears below your item title in the search-results page. If the 55-character limit of a title doesn't do justice to your item, buy the subtitle upgrade and

Macintosh G3 Powerbook Pismo, 500MHz Firewire
256MB RAM, 60GB drive, with USB Trackball!

use it to further describe your item: size, shape, color, tech specs, extra accessories, and so on. And if you insist on hyping your item—*Must see! One of a kind!*—a subtitle lets you do so without wasting precious title space. In all, subtitles are a great way to get a searcher's attention and set your auction apart. **Note:** When writing a subtitle, don't obsess too much on keywords. The content of a subtitle isn't searched when a user does a standard, title-only search. Subtitles are searched, however, when a user searches within the title and description.

Formatting with HTML: The Basics

If you're looking for instructions on how to give your listings scrolling ticker-tape text and glitzy background graphics, you picked up the wrong book.

When it comes to formatting auction text, we take a conservative stance: you should use a minimum of text formatting in your listings.

Why are we raining on your design parade? A few reasons, starting with the nature of eBay itself. eBay listings aren't design galleries—they're closer to classified ads. Imagine if your daily newspaper allowed classified ad buyers to format their ads any way they wanted. The classifieds wouldn't be all that easy to read, would they?

Another reason is that fancy layouts take more time to load and often don't display properly on some browsers. Why run the risk of turning away customers?

And finally, we've never seen a shred of evidence proving that fancy formatting attracts higher bids than plain formatting. In fact, many buyers are turned off by fancy formatting. Who would you rather buy a used car from: someone who shouted at you and was wearing plaid pants, a polka-dotted jacket, and a big red bowtie, or someone in a conservative suit who calmly gave you the information you needed to make a buying decision? We thought so.

When it comes to eBay listings, simpler is better. More to the point, simpler sells.

HTML Basics

As we said on page 38, HTML stands for *hypertext markup language*, and is a set of text codes, called *tags*, that allow you to format text for the Web.

HTML is extremely simple, at least the way we recommend you use it. Here is some simple formatting and the HTML codes behind it.

Many tags come in pairs: you "turn on" some formatting, and then "turn off" the formatting by *closing* the tag. A closing tag has a forward slash (/) in it. Shown here: the <b> tag pair, which formats text in bold.

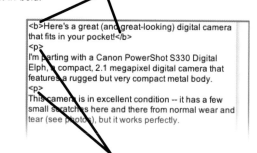

```
<b>Here's a great (and great-looking) digital camera
that fits in your pocket!</b>
<p>
I'm parting with a Canon PowerShot S330 Digital
Elph, a compact, 2.1 megapixel digital camera that
features a rugged but very compact metal body.
<p>
This camera is in excellent condition -- it has a few
small scratches here and there from normal wear and
tear (see photos), but it works perfectly.
```

On page 85, we recommended starting new paragraphs frequently. Here's how: simply put the <p> tag between the two paragraphs. That's right: Web browsers aren't smart enough to tell that you pressed Return a couple of times to start a new paragraph. You must literally spell paragraphs out using the <p> tag.

Here's how the code above displays.

Here's a great (and great-looking) digital camera that fits in your pocket!

I'm parting with a Canon PowerShot S330 Digital Elph, a compact, 2.1 megapixel digital camera that features a rugged but very compact metal body.

This camera is in excellent condition -- it has a few small scratches here and there from normal wear and tear (see photos), but it works perfectly.

Tip: Write first, format later. To avoid typos and brain strain, write your description first, then go back and add formatting.

The Basic Tags You Need

There are dozens of HTML tags and even more ways to employ them. But for eBay, you need only a handful.

When you want...	Use...	Example
A new paragraph	<p>	This is one paragraph. <p> This is another.
A large, bold heading	<h3> and </h3>	<h3>Brand-new Apple iPod</h3>
Italic text	<i> and </i>	A <i>great</i> book.
A bulleted list	<ul> and </ul> at the start and end of the list; <li> before each line	Features include: <p> <ul> <li>250 watts output <li>3D graphics <li>built-in pockets </ul>
To center text (Note: avoid centering long passages of text.)	<center> and </center>	<center>This is centered</center>
A line break without an extra space between lines	 	This is one line. This line is right below it.
Draw a horizontal line across the page	<hr>	This is a heading <hr> And my description starts here.
Change the type font	<font> and </font>	<font face="Verdana, Arial, Helvetica">This is a san-serif font</font>
Link to a page on another Web site	<a href>	See page 88.
Link to a self-hosted picture	<img>	See page 89.

Putting it All Together

Combining Tags

At times, you may need to combine, or *nest*, tags—for example, to create a bold, centered heading. The only trick to this is that you should close tags in the order opposite from how you opened them.

Correct:
The Bold and the Centered

Incorrect:
The Bold and the Centered

Truth be told, most Web browsers will still display the incorrect version properly, but it's better to be safe.

Linking to Other Web Pages

To add a link to another Web page—perhaps to a manufacturer's page or to a review describing your item—use the <a> tag. The following example creates a link to eBay's home page.

<a href="http://www.eBay.com">Go to eBay</a>

Tip: Be sure to test any links before your auction goes live. Use the Preview Description link in the Title & Description page to view your description as it will appear. Any links you've added will be fully operational in the preview window—click to test them. Alternatively, you can save your description as a plain-text file and end its name with *.html*, then open this file in your Web browser.

To Learn More

eBay's online help and community forums are great places to learn more about HTML. If you'd like a reference book, we recommend the *HTML for the World Wide Web Visual QuickStart Guide* series, from Peachpit Press.

Putting Them Together

Here's a complete listing that uses most of these tags. To save space here, we've left out our shipping and payment policies, but you will, of course, want to include your versions of them in your descriptions.

<h3>Here's a great (and great-looking) digital camera that fits in your pocket!</h3>
<p>
After taking thousands of great shots with it, I'm parting with my Canon PowerShot S330 Digital Elph, a compact digital camera that features a rugged but very compact metal body.
<p>
Features include:
<ul>
<li>2.1 megapixel resolution
<li>1.5-inch LCD screen
<li>Direct-printing capability for Canon printers -- print pictures straight from the camera without having to transfer to your computer first
</ul>
Read a review of this camera <a href="http://www.dpreview.com/reviews/canondigitalixus330/">here.</a>
<p>
This camera is 18 months old and is in excellent condition -- it has a few small scratches here and there from normal wear and tear (see photos), but it works perfectly.
<p>
I don't have the ori[ginal]
including: USB cabl[e]
ware for Windows a[nd]

Here's a great (and great-looking) digital camera that fits in your pocket!

After taking thousands of great shots with it, I'm parting with my Canon PowerShot S330 Digital Elph, a compact digital camera that features a rugged but very compact metal body.

Features include:

- 2.1 megapixel resolution
- 1.5-inch LCD screen
- Direct-printing capability for Canon printers -- print pictures straight from the camera without having to transfer to your computer first

Read a review of this camera here.

This camera is 18 months old and is in excellent condition -- it has a few small scratches here and there from normal wear and tear (see photos), but it works perfectly.

I don't have the original box, but I will include all factory-supplied accessories, including: USB cable, rechargeable battery, battery charger, manual, and software for Windows and Mac.

Linking to Self-Hosted Pictures

If you're hosting your own pictures, use the <img> tag to add them to your item description, like so:

`<img src="http://myserver.com/poodle_bench.jpg" height="400" width="300">`

Place the correct address for your Web server here.

Avoid using spaces or most special characters in your picture names.

The height and width attributes are optional, but recommended—they'll help your listing page display a bit faster by allowing the browser to position the text even as the pictures continue to load. The values are in pixels—you may recall that we recommended you jot them down when preparing your images (page 79).

Getting fancier. If you'd like your description text to flow around an image, add an *align* attribute to the tag:

`<img src="http://myserver.com/ladybugs.jpg" height="400" width="300" align="left">`

The image will appear along the left edge of the browser window and the text will flow around it. Use align="right" to right-align the image.

Handmade Ceramic Bowl Candy Dish with Ladybugs!

This brightly colored, handmade bowl is both whimsical and useful.

The bowl is approximately 6 inches wide and stands 3 inches tall. The bowl is 2 inches deep at its center.

The interior of the bowl is a bright orange and the exterior is bright pink. The rim of the bowl is gold and the feet are a bright red/orange.

This item is in excellent condition. There are no nicks or imperfections in the paint or the ceramic.

CHAPTER 5

Managing Your Auctions

Auction Management at a Glance

Your work isn't over when your auction goes live. Quite the contrary—you're open for business, and it's time to be on the alert.

You'll want to be checking the status of your auction to see how the bidding is going. You may receive emails from potential bidders who have questions that need answers. You may need to revise your listing to include more information about your item or to correct an error. You may even need to play the role of cyber-security guard by canceling a bid made by a potentially untrustworthy buyer.

Bottom line: Once your auction is underway, you can't just walk away and wait for the money to come in. Your responsiveness at this stage plays a big role in your success as a seller and can significantly affect your feedback rating.

Here's an introduction to the topics we address in this chapter.

Tracking Your Progress

Are people bidding? Are they even looking? You'll want to keep an eye on your auction as it progresses. You can do this several ways, starting with simply visiting the listing page itself (page 94). You can also sign up to receive daily status emails that detail the progress of your auctions (page 94). And the My eBay feature is a superb tool for auction management (page 95).

Editing Your Listing

As your auction progresses, you may want to change your listing—to address a frequently asked question, for example, or in the hope of jump-starting slow bidding. You can add information, change images, and even change your pricing, but timing is everything—the changes you can make depend on whether your listing has any bids and when your auction ends (page 96).

Ending an Auction Early

Although you'll almost always allow an auction to run its course, there may be times when you need to end it early. For example, maybe your item was broken or lost and is no longer available. If you can't complete an auction, you can put it out of its misery (page 101).

Managing Bids and Bidders

Numerous bidder-related chores may need your attention as your auction runs. Potential bidders may have questions about your item or shipping policies; you'll want to respond promptly. You can also cancel a bid if it's from someone with whom you've had trouble in the past or who has an alarming number of negative comments in his or her feedback profile. You can also block specific bidders as well as pre-approve them. You'll find all the details on pages 98–101.

No Sale? Relisting an Item

Although we're giving you our best ingredients for a winning auction recipe, many auctions end without a winning bidder. It's often worth trying again by reworking your auction and relisting your item (page 102).

Power Tools for Auction Automation

If you conduct a modest number of auctions—maybe a few per week—you'll probably be content with the basic auction-management features we'll be discussing in this chapter. But if your auctioneering grows to encompass dozens of simultaneous auctions, you may want to investigate the many software packages and Web services that are available for creating, managing, and automating auctions.

Auction software talks directly to eBay, bypassing the eBay Web pages that we've explored in previous chapters. You use the software to create listings—maybe hundreds of them, if you like—and the software communicates with eBay to make them happen.

Auction-management software can also create detailed status reports that show you what's selling, to whom, and when. Most programs can also print shipping labels and packing slips, generate response emails to bidders, and help you track insertion and final-value fees.

eBay itself has created several auction-automation programs that streamline listing and tracking auctions. They include Turbo Lister, Selling Manager, and Selling Manager Pro (see page 146). Hoping to hitch a ride on eBay's platinum-plated bandwagon, many third-party companies have also gotten into the act (see page 148).

Most auction tools are available for Windows computers only, but some excellent ones are also available for the Apple Macintosh. And some tools are Web-based, and thus work well on both platforms.

Most of these programs or services cost money, so be sure they're worth the convenience to you. Be sure to factor in these additional costs when deciding whether to automate your auctions.

Tracking Your Progress

Now that the horse is out of the gate, you need to keep an eye on the race. You may want to monitor traffic to your auction page to see if you need to make any of the tweaks we describe on the following pages. And you'll certainly want to monitor bidding in anticipation of your pending riches.

You can track the progress of your auctions in several ways. You can simply go to the listing page itself, you can sign up to receive daily status emails that detail all your buying and selling activity, and you can use My eBay to monitor multiple auctions at once.

Regardless of how you locate your listing, once you get there, look it over. Are there any bids? What does the counter at the bottom of the page say? Are people looking? If the action seems lukewarm, you may want to fine-tune your auction. Or you may simply have a lukewarm item.

Let's watch the bids come in.

Viewing the Listing

The easiest way to see what's happening in an auction is to go to its listing page. This is also a good way to see who's bidding and to check on his or her feedback.

How do you find your listing? There are a few ways.

My eBay. A great way to keep tabs on all your selling activities is with the powerful and free My eBay (opposite page).

Your confirmation email. If you've used My eBay to sign up for a listing confirmation email (see page 15), you'll find a link to the listing in that same email. To check out the listing page, click that link.

Bookmark the listing. When you submit a new listing, eBay displays a link to the listing's page. We'll often click on that link to go to the listing, and then bookmark the page. (To avoid cluttering up your bookmarks or favorites list, remember to delete the bookmark when the auction ends and you've been paid.)

Do a search. If you didn't bookmark the listing or receive a confirmation email, you can always do a search. In fact, this is a good way to see if any competing listings have shown up since you created yours.

Daily Status Updates

Want a daily tally of how things are going? Let eBay do the work. One of the many automatic notifications you can choose to receive from eBay is a daily email that details your ongoing sales and buying activity.

These messages contain details on your current auctions, along with helpful links and tips. eBay often describes new features in these notifications, so subscribing to them is a good way to keep up to date with eBay itself.

To sign up for these reports, use the steps described on page 15. But truth be told, we don't find these daily email updates to be terribly reliable. The information tends to be hours old and not the late-breaking news we're looking for to help us track our auctions.

My eBay's "All Selling" Display

If you're like us, you want up-to-the-minute information on how your auctions are progressing, and you want to access this information many times a day.

This is where My eBay becomes essential. Click on the All Selling link, and you get details on items you're selling, items you've sold, and more.

Get an at-a-glance look at how your auctions are faring.

What's coming up? When you create auctions with a delayed start time (see page 40), they appear here until that time arrives.

What didn't sell? Auctions that ended without winning bidders appear here, where you can relist them.

Things to do: this area lists chores you need to perform, such as leaving feedback and answering questions.

How are your current auctions doing?

To view a specific listing page, click its title.

Green is good: if an auction's current price is green, it means that a bidder has met your starting price (or reserve).

You can customize the All Selling page and change the order in which each section is displayed.

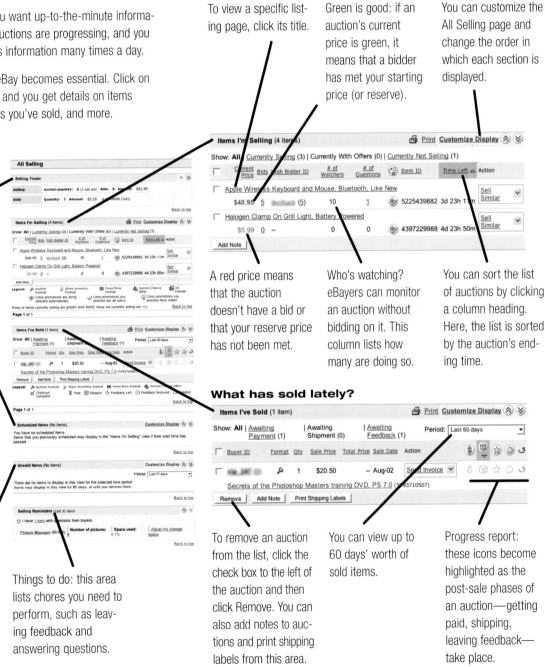

A red price means that the auction doesn't have a bid or that your reserve price has not been met.

Who's watching? eBayers can monitor an auction without bidding on it. This column lists how many are doing so.

You can sort the list of auctions by clicking a column heading. Here, the list is sorted by the auction's ending time.

What has sold lately?

To remove an auction from the list, click the check box to the left of the auction and then click Remove. You can also add notes to auctions and print shipping labels from this area.

You can view up to 60 days' worth of sold items.

Progress report: these icons become highlighted as the post-sale phases of an auction—getting paid, shipping, leaving feedback—take place.

Changing an Existing Auction

Your auction for The Enchanted Broccoli Forest cookbook is up and running, but you forgot to mention those yam stains on page 57. Or perhaps a potential bidder has contacted you with a question you think should be addressed in the listing. Or maybe bidding is off to a slow start and you want to add some listing options to spice up the auction page.

These are just a few of the good reasons to add or change the description of your item, change some listing options, alter the duration of your auction, or tweak any of the other details we've covered.

As your auction progresses, the kinds of changes you can make become more limited. A brand-new auction with no bids? You can change almost everything. An auction with a bid and an hour to go? You can't change much.

As for making the actual changes, the process is straightforward. You'll use those same pages we encountered back in Chapter 2: the Title & Description page, the Pictures & Details page, and so on.

What You Can Change, and When

What kinds of changes can you make? It depends on how far along the auction is.

Does the auction have any bids?

YES

NO

Does the auction end within twelve hours?

YES

NO

You can change any aspect of your listing except for the selling format. For example, if you initially chose to sell your item at an online auction, you can't switch to a fixed-price auction now. But the sky's the limit for making other additions, deletions, or edits.

It's late in the game. At this point, you can only add to your listing options—for example, add a gallery photo or one of those gimmicky design themes. Hey, eBay never met a listing fee it didn't like, and is happy to collect them right up to the very end.

You can add to your item description, add a second category, lower or remove your reserve price (page 104), or add listing options. At this point, you can't change the original item description—you can only add to it. (In the Revise Your Item page, click the Add to Description link next to the Title & Description heading.) You can add additional text, including HTML formatting tags, as well as links to photos that you are hosting (see page 89).

On the listing page, the additions to your item description will appear below the original description, along with the date and time of your revision.

Making Changes

Here's how to make the changes. Be sure to sign in before performing the following steps.

Step 1. Go to the auction's page.

Get there by clicking the auction's link in the Selling area of My eBay or by using the other techniques described on page 94. (If you're using My eBay, you can eliminate a step by choosing the Revise command from the drop-down menu in the Action column.)

Step 2. On the auction page, click the Revise Your Item link.

New Coach Signature cell phone case
You are signed in
Seller status: Your item has one bid

Revise your item
Promote your item
Sell a similar item

The Revise Your Item: Review & Submit Listing page appears. This page resembles the Review & Submit page you mulled over when creating your auction (page 56).

Step 3. Make the changes

To change an item, scroll to its corresponding area of the page and click the appropriate link. For example, to add to your payment and shipping details, click the Add Payment & Shipping link.

Step 4. Click the Save Changes button at the bottom of the page.

The Review & Submit page appears. To make additional changes, repeat Steps 3 and 4. Do one last round of proof-reading, then check out the bottom of the page, where eBay lists any additional fees your changes may involve.

Step 5. Click the Submit Revisions button.

If you want to start again, click the Cancel Revision button instead.

You can't keep changes a secret. Potential bidders will see a new link next to your auction's Description heading.

Description (revised) This link leads to a page that tells viewers what was changed and when.

Item Revisions summary for item #5793710507

The seller has revised the following item information:

Date	Time	Revised Information
Jul-30-05	14:04:55 PDT	Description

Managing Bids and Bidders

While your auction is underway, you may need to deal with bids and the people who make them. Bidders or potential bidders may email with questions that need prompt answers. If you're having problems with a bidder, you may have to take the drastic step of canceling a bid—or the even more drastic step of blocking a bidder from your auctions. In some cases, you may even decide to end an auction early.

These are all straightforward tasks, but as with so many things eBay, elements of diplomacy and community relations are involved. Here's a look at the basics behind bid management.

To perform some of the tasks we describe here, you use the Bid History page. True to its name, the Bid History page lists the trail of bids for a particular auction. Bids that have been retracted or canceled also appear here.

To view an auction's Bid History page (bottom), click this link.

Answering Questions

Although your email address isn't visible on your listing page, other eBayers can still contact you by email. On your item's listing page, eBay members can click the Ask Seller a Question link in the Seller Information area. This displays a form that allows inquiring minds to submit a question that arrives in your email. (The question also appears in the My Messages area of My eBay; see page 28.)

This querying ability lets bidders or potential bidders contact you with questions: Does your *Best of "Bewitched"* DVD include the new Darren or the old one? It's your job to answer all reasonable questions quickly and courteously. In fact, it's good business to also answer the unreasonable questions.

When responding through eBay's site, you can, among other things, choose to post the question, along with your response, on the listing page. You might do this if you anticipate receiving similar questions.

Contacting Bidders

Although you rarely have reason to contact bidders while an auction is active, you can. Perhaps you've perused your high bidder's feedback profile and you're curious about some recent complaints. To contact the current high bidder, click his or her User ID. A new page appears containing the high bidder's Member Profile. Click the Contact Member button. Compose your email on the next page and click the Send button. The bidder receives your message via email and in his or her My Messages Inbox. (**Tip:** If you'd like to see members' email addresses displayed next to their User IDs, go to My eBay and click the Preferences link in the My Account area. Scroll down to Other General Preferences, then click its Show link. Click the Yes box next to Show User IDs with Email Addresses, then click Apply.)

You can also contact any of the bidders who have participated in the auction. On the auction's Bid History page (left), click on the ID of the user you want to contact.

At the end of an auction, you can view the email addresses of all bidders for 14 days. On the Bid History page, click the Show Email Addresses link. Remember, it's against eBay's rules to compile email addresses for your own spamming—er, marketing—purposes.

I Take it Back: Retracted Bids

Bidders can retract bids under very limited circumstances. If someone typed in the wrong amount when bidding—$1,000 instead of $100—he or she can retract the bid and immediately type the correct amount.

A bidder can also retract a bid if you've changed your item description substantially during the course of the auction. And finally, if a bidder has tried to get in touch with you via email and those emails have been returned—they've *bounced back*, in email jargon—he or she may retract a bid.

Only under these circumstances can a bid be legitimately retracted. Bid retraction is serious business—it can completely disrupt an auction. For this reason, eBay keeps track of the number of bids that a user retracts in any six-month period. This number appears in the user's feedback profile.

When a bid is retracted, eBay adds a comment to this effect to the auction's bid history.

I Don't Want Your Business: Canceling a Bid

You can cancel a bid at any time, but you should never do so lightly. As with bid retraction, bid cancellation is serious business. eBay won't list your bid cancellations in your feedback profile, but there can be repercussions if bidders complain about a pattern of cancellations.

There are a few circumstances under which you might cancel a bid. If you've tried unsuccessfully to contact a bidder or if a bidder has consistently negative feedback, it's reasonable to steer clear of that person—eBay doesn't require you put yourself in the line of fire when doing business.

Canceling a bid as a favor. When a bidder retracts a bid, the retraction is reflected in his or her feedback. Because of this, a bidder may contact you and ask that you cancel his or her bid so that he or she doesn't have to retract it. You're under no obligation to do so, but if you're feeling charitable—and if the bidder is making a reasonable request—go ahead and cancel the bid. You should try to do this as long before the close of the auction as possible in order to give other bidders a chance to step up to the plate.

How to Cancel a Bid

To cancel a bid, you must fill out the Bid Cancellation page, and to do *that*, you need to know your auction's item number.

Go to the item's listing page and locate the item number. Write it down or, better yet, select it with your mouse and then choose Copy from your browser's Edit menu.

Next, click on the Site Map link at the top of the page. Under Selling Activities, you'll find a link named Cancel Bids on Your Listing. Click this link, and the Bid Cancellation page appears.

Tip: As an alternative to going to your listing page to get the item number, you can customize My eBay to display item numbers in the All Selling area; see page 95.

What: Type or paste the auction's item number.

Who: Type the User ID of the member whose bid you want to cancel.

Why: Specify the reason you're canceling the bid.

Canceling bids placed on your listing

Bids should only be canceled for good reasons (see examples). Remember, canceled bids cannot be restored.

Enter information about your listing below and click Cancel Bid.

6789930350
Item number

User ID of the bid you are cancelling

Reason for cancellation:

(80 characters or less)

cancel bid   clear form

Bid retraction and cancellation history

User ID	Action / Explanation	Date of Bid and Retraction
~~xxxxxx~~ (1)	Cancelled: US $5.20 Explanation: Placed bid by mistake	Bid: Jul-31-05 10:14:18 PDT Cancelled: Jul-31-05 10:15:49 PDT

To cancel the bid, click Cancel Bid. To start over, click Clear Form.

Cancelled bids can't be reinstated.

The number of bids on your auction will be reduced by one and the cancellation will be listed in the item's bid history.

Advanced Bidder and Auction Management

Let's continue our look at bidder and auction management by examining some of the more obscure chores you may need to perform.

And Don't Come Back: Blocking a Bidder

Perhaps you've run across a good-for-nothing bidder and you refuse to do business with him again. You can block him—and any other undesirables—from bidding on your future auctions.

Step 1. To block a bidder, click this link.

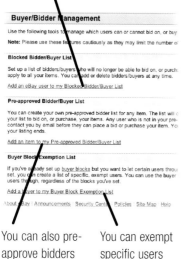

You can also pre-approve bidders and buyers for a specific auction, as described at right.

You can exempt specific users from any of your buyer blocks.

Begin by going to the eBay site map. Then, under Selling Activities, click the Block Bidder/Buyer List link. The Bidder/Buyer Management page appears.

Step 2. Type the User ID or email address of each bidder you want to block. You can place each entry on a separate line as we've done here, or separate entries with a space, comma, or semicolon (;).

Step 3. Click Submit.

To remove a bidder from your blacklist—perhaps he has made up for his prior transgression—return to the page above, delete the bidder's User ID or email address from the list, and then click Submit again.

Members Only: Creating a Pre-Approved Bidder List

If you want to be very exclusive about who can participate in a particular auction, you can create a list of pre-approved bidders who will be the only eBayers allowed to bid on that item. If people who aren't on your pre-approved list attempt to bid, they will be asked to contact you in order to place their bids. If you want to enable those users to bid, you can add their User IDs or email addresses to your pre-approved list.

Why shut out most of eBay's members? Maybe you've developed a devoted following of buyers for your snuff tin collectibles, and you want to create an auction for them alone. Or maybe you're conducting an auction on behalf of a club, and you want only its members to be able to bid.

To create a pre-approved list for an auction, first create the auction listing as you normally would. Jot down the auction's item number or copy it to your computer's Clipboard—you'll need the item number later.

Next, go to the Bidder/Buyer Management page and click the Pre-Approved Bidder/Buyer List link. Your browser will load the page shown at right.

Step 1. To create a pre-approved bidder list for a specific auction, click this link.

Pre-Approve Bidders/Buyers

Create your own pre-approved bidder/buyer list for any item and only allow those on your list to bid or buy. Any bidder/buyer who is not in your list will be asked to contact you by email to place a bid or buy your item. You can add or delete bidders/buyers up until your listing ends.
Please use this feature cautiously as it may limit the number of bids or sales of your item.

Items with Pre-Approved Bidders
Currently, you have no items with pre-approved bidders

+ Add a new item with pre-approved bidders

Step 2. Specify the item number and User IDs.

Pre-Approve Bidders/Buyers

Add Item

1. Enter the item number you'd like to restrict to pre-approved bidders/buyers. You can copy your item number from My eBay in the Selling tab or from your item page.
2. Add your approved bidders/buyers in the box below. View tips to pre-approve your bidders/buyers.

Type or paste the auction's item number here.

Type each pre-approved bidder's User ID, pressing the Return or Enter key after each one. (You can also separate each ID with a comma.)

Step 3. Click Submit Item.

Game Over: Ending an Auction Early

Generally, you should let an auction run its course. But at times you may have to end an auction early. Maybe you knocked your Yellow Submarine lava lamp off the table and it shattered on the floor. (At least you'll find out what that lava stuff really is.) Or maybe you've been called out of town suddenly and won't be around to ship the item after it sells.

To end your listing early, go to the All Selling area of My eBay. Jot down or copy the item number for the auction you want to end. Next, go to the eBay site map and, under Selling Activities, click the End Your Listing link. A page appears asking for the item number of your auction. Type or paste the item number in the box and click Continue.

What happens next depends on whether your auction has any bids. (But no matter what, eBay still charges you for the item's listing fee.)

No bids? If there are no bids, you're taken to a page where you can choose one of several reasons for ending your auction.

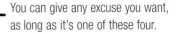

End My Listing Early

Select a reason for ending your listing early. The reason will appear on the Closed Item page.

○ The item is no longer available for sale.
○ There was an error in the starting price or reserve amount.
○ There was an error in the listing.
○ The item was lost or broken.

End My Listing

You can give any excuse you want, as long as it's one of these four.

After you've chosen the reason, click End My Listing.

Bids? If your auction does have bids, you'll need to either cancel all existing bids or sell to the current high bidder.

If your item is broken or otherwise unavailable, you'll need to cancel bids. The End My Listing Early page shown at lower left appears, where you can choose the reason for ending the auction.

Tip: In the interest of good customer service, consider sending an email to each of your bidders to further explain why you ended your auction.

If you want to end the auction and sell the item to the current high bidder, click Sell Item.

No Sale: Relisting an Item

You've carefully performed each step, taken our advice, and followed your instincts. And despite your good intentions, the virtual gavel has slammed and your auction has ended without a sale.

Don't feel bad. It isn't unusual for an auction to end with no bids or with the reserve price unmet. But eBay has a heart—you can relist your auction without paying an additional insertion fee, provided you do so within 90 days.

That doesn't mean relisting is free. If you opted for extra-cost listing options, such as multiple photos or a gallery photo, you'll have to pay for those options the second time around. And of course, eBay will charge a final-value fee if your relisted item sells.

Technically, eBay charges you the insertion fee the second time. If the relisted auction is successful, however, the insertion fee is refunded. If the second auction is also unsuccessful, eBay won't refund the second insertion fee—eBay doesn't want to encourage the continuous relisting of items that don't sell. If you think the third time will be the charm, you'll have to pay for the privilege of finding out.

To be eligible for relisting, you must meet certain criteria, which we've summarized at right. If you meet these criteria, you can relist with a few mouse clicks—although you may also want to put some work into refining the new listing so that it attracts the action you're hoping for.

Can You Relist?

Is your failed auction eligible for relisting? To find out, answer each of the following questions. If you can answer "yes" to each one, then you can relist.

For No-Reserve Auctions

- Did the auction receive no bids?

- Are you willing to relist at the same or lower starting price?

- Can you relist within 90 days of the failed auction's closing?

For Reserve Auctions

- Was the reserve price not met?

- Are you willing to relist at the same or lower reserve price or to remove the reserve price entirely?

- Can you relist within 90 days of the failed auction's closing?

How to Relist

One way to relist is by going to the failed auction's listing page. Near the top of the page, you'll see a Relist link. Click this link, and you'll see the Relist Your Item page shown below. You can also relist through My eBay; in the All Selling area, click the Unsold link.

Suggestion box: eBay often suggests changes based on similar (but successful) auctions. If you like a recommendation, click its Edit link to go to the appropriate part of the Sell Your Item form.

What next?

That depends on how much corrective surgery you feel your auction needs.

After you've made your changes, review the bottom of the Review & Submit Listing page. If you added any listing upgrades, their additional fees will be listed there.

To...	Do this...
Relist without making any changes at all (usually not a good idea)	Scroll to the bottom of the Relist Your Item: Review & Submit Listing page and click the Submit Listing button.
Change the item's category or add a second category	Click the Change Main Category or Add Second Category links, then choose categories as described on pages 36–37.
Step through each of the main listing-creation pages, making changes along the way	Click the listing-editing links near the top of the page or use the Back button at the bottom of the page to step backwards through each listing-editing page.
Make changes in one area, such as the title and description	Click the link for the appropriate area. (For example, to tweak the title and description, click the Title & Description link.)
Change the selling format (for example, to change from a conventional online auction to a fixed-price auction)	Click the Edit Listing Format link, and then choose the desired format.

Make it Better the Second Time Around

Relisting after a failed attempt? Here are some tips for how you might improve your auction the second time around.

Revamp the title, description, or category. Did you give potential bidders enough information in the right place? Look at some successful auctions (see page 19) and see if you may have overlooked any important search keywords, and make sure you haven't listed your item in an inappropriate or obscure category. Be sure your description adequately describes your item's irresistible qualities. And remove extraneous text from the description. Don't force bidders to wade through advertising or legal mumbo jumbo in order to find the information that will inspire them to bid.

Add pictures. Pictures can never hurt an auction. The only downsides are the additional work it takes to capture, pre-pare, and upload the images, and the extra fees you may be assessed.

Get rid of that reserve price. We've said it before: we encourage you to list items without a reserve price. That magical "NR" (no reserve) in an auction's title may entice previously hesitant bidders to look. Do your homework and set your starting bid within your comfort zone, then forego the reserve. If you must set a reserve price for a valuable item, consider putting the reserve price into the item description to deflect possible bidder frustration.

Expand your payment options. If you previously accepted only checks and money orders, consider adding an instant-payment option, such as PayPal. Conversely, if you restricted payment to PayPal only, consider opening up your options by also taking checks or money orders.

More Auction-Management Tips

Have Another?
Relisting Successful Auctions or Similar Items

On the previous pages, we described how to relist an item if it doesn't sell. It's worth noting that you can also relist a *successful* auction if you have more than one of whatever you sold. Let's say you just sold your Leonard Nimoy bobble head and you discovered a second identical one in your closet. By relisting the first auction, you can put the second bobble head up for sale in a flash.

Go to My eBay, locate the successful auction in the Items I've Sold list, and select Relist from the Action drop-down menu. (As shown at right, the Action menu gives you one-click access to many auction-related chores.)

Be sure to make any changes to the new auction to reflect the duplicate item you're listing; unless the items you're listing are brand new, it's unlikely they're identical. When you relist a successful auction, eBay will charge all fees, including the insertion fee, for the relisted auction.

A variation on this theme involves listing an item similar to one that you currently have up for auction. Near the top of the item's page, you'll see a link called Sell Similar. Click it, and you'll be taken to the category-selection page.

You can also sell a similar item by going to the Items I'm Selling area of My eBay's All Selling page and clicking on an item's Sell Similar link, which you'll find in the Action drop-down menu.

Tip: You can save a lot of time when creating a new listing by using the "sell similar" feature. When you use this feature, eBay fills out each of the main auction-creation pages for you based on the existing auction. You need only change the information that's different about the new item.

To open the Action drop-down menu, click the arrow.

Help! eBay Ended
My Auction

You check your email and find a notice that eBay has removed a listing early. Perhaps eBay feels that the item falls into one of the prohibited categories we've outlined here. Or maybe eBay was contacted by a VeRO member (see page 9) who alleges that your listing infringes on a copyright or trademark.

What to do? First of all, don't simply re-list the item. Your account could be suspended and you might be sued or even prosecuted. If you disagree with your listing's cancellation, you have some recourse. Go to the following Help page, which provides an overview of early cancellations: www.ebay.com/help/confidence/listing-ended.html.

This page contains links that allow you to, in essence, appeal eBay's decision. If eBay agrees with you, you can relist the item. Alas, our research suggests that you're unlikely to have success appealing eBay's decision to end an auction early.

More About Reserve
Price Adjustments

Page 97 noted that you can lower or remove an auction's reserve price, provided that the auction doesn't end within 12 hours.

If your auction already has bids, lowering your reserve price has additional implications that can be confusing. We don't recommend adjusting your reserve price on auctions that are already running; it can confuse bidders and disrupt the auction. But if you're interested in the details, see www.ebay.com/help/sell/lowering-reserve.html.

Getting More Out of Your Andale Counters

Those counters at the bottom of your auctions aren't just sitting there chalking up visitors. Andale compiles this information and creates statistics that are available to you at no charge.

Beneath the counter on your listing page is a link called FREE Counters and Services from Andale.

00080
FREE Counters and Services from Andale

All of your active auctions appear here, whether you've chosen to add a counter to them or not.

To view your reports, click this link. You'll need to register and work your way through some advertising screens (what did you expect for free?), but once you do, you'll arrive at your Start page. At the top of the page is a pop-up menu named Andale Quicklinks; to view your counter statistics, choose Counters.

View auctions that have ended in the last 30 days.

There's More, But It'll Cost You

A counter-statistics report contains a wealth of additional options—and most of them cost money. When you click one of these appealing-looking links (View Report), you'll be taken to an advertising page that describes the goodie at hand. To get the goods, you'll need to subscribe to one or a combination of Andale's auction-management tools (see page 148). For example, you won't be able to see your hit details by hour or by day unless you upgrade beyond Andale's free service.

Green numbers indicate an above-average number of hits. Congrats—you're doing something right.

Red numbers indicate a below-average number of hits. (Andale calculates the average based on your item's category.) If the auction is still active, maybe it's time to consider some cosmetic surgery to see if you can pick up the pace (see page 96).

You can customize a counter style. If you must have the numbers in your counters look like Easter eggs or firecrackers, this is the place to do it. You can choose from a wide variety of styles and other options.

All Items	Live Items	Completed Items				Hits:	Above Avg	**Average**	Below Avg

Items With Counters | Items Without Counters | Items With Bids/Sales | All Item Details   Time Zone: [Pacific Time ▼]

Items I'm Selling (5)   Hits by Hour | Hits by Day

☑All		Item	High Bidder	Time Left	Current Price	Hits	Bids	Qty	Hit Details
☐	5793710507	Secrets of the Photoshop Masters training DVD, PS 7.0		20h 6m	$4.95	22	1	1	🗁 View Report
	Auto Relist this item Add Andale Checkout List a similar item								
☐	5794999614	Secrets of the Photoshop Masters training DVD, PS 7.0	--	23h 44m	$19.95	--	0		Add Counter
	Auto Relist this item Add Andale Checkout List a similar item								
☐	6789930350	New Coach Signature cell phone case, gray/white NR		3d 1h+	$16.99	48	3	1	🗁 View Report
	Auto Relist this item Add Andale Checkout List a similar item								
☐	5225439882	Apple Wireless Keyboard and Mouse, Bluetooth, Like New		3d 2h+	$76.00	82	10	1	🗁 View Report
	Auto Relist this item Add Andale Checkout List a similar item								
☐	4397229988	Halogen Clamp On Grill Light, Battery Powered	--	4d 3h+	$5.99	3		1	🗁 View Report
	Auto Relist this item Add Andale Checkout List a similar item								

Totals (5 items)					Current Price	Hits	Bids	Qty
All Items Listed:					$ 123.88	**155**	14	5
Items With Bids/Sales:					$ 97.94	**152**	14	3

[Add Counter...] [Edit Counter Style...] [Reset Counter]

You can add a counter to an auction that doesn't have one.

Choose Counter Style and Options

Digit Style:	[Nature -> ▼] [Scotties ▼]	𝟙 𝟚 𝟛
Counter Type:	⦿ Unique Views (Recommended. Doesn't count consecutive refreshes by same buyer)	
	◯ Page Views (Counts every time the page is refreshed)	
Options:	☑ Border	
	☑ Use this style as my default counter style	

[Back] [Edit Counters]

CHAPTER 6

Sold!

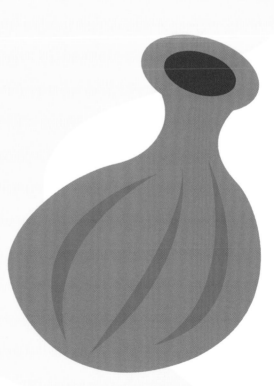

After the Sale: The Big Picture

Your auction has ended and you have a winning bidder. Now's the time for the relationship between seller and buyer to begin: you contact the buyer, iron out any payment and shipping details, ship the item once you've been paid, and leave feedback for the buyer.

As you can see, you and the buyer each have responsibilities. The buyer needs to pay promptly and in the manner you have designated. And you need to put your mouth where your newfound money is. Once you've been paid, you need to deliver the goods—and ideally, the sooner, the better. Prompt, courteous service is always important, but it's particularly critical if you're a new seller seeking to build a solid record of positive feedback.

That's the overall process, and it takes place tens of thousands of times every day. Now and then, something may go wrong. A winning bidder may not respond, or an item may arrive damaged. Don't panic. Most people are reasonable, and there's usually a way to resolve problems.

It's time to take action.

Contact the Buyer

As soon as the auction ends, send a clear, concise, courteous email with key information reiterating details about payment, shipping, and other logistics (page 110).

New Coach Signature cell phone case, gray/white NR

✓ **Your item sold for US $36.50!**
Buyer's email:
Buyer's Postal Code: 90740

Send Invoice >
To send your buyer payment information, click the **Send Invoice** button.

Getting Paid

For a seller, this is what it's all about: you'll receive payment in your chosen form. If you're using PayPal (page 54), you'll give up some of the payment (convenience has a price).

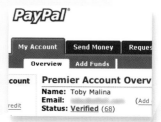

Give Feedback

The deal is done and you're delighted; now's the time to tell the world by distilling your experience with the buyer into a maximum of 80 characters (page 112). If you're having problems with the transaction, try to resolve them before leaving feedback. Remember, flames can come back to burn you (see page 114).

User ID:	myfeggi				Show all transactions
Item Number:	6789930350				
Rating:	⦿ Positive	○ Neutral	○ Negative	○ I will leave feedback later	
Comment:	Great buyer. Lightning-fast payment. Recommend highly. Thanks!				
	18 characters left				

Keep the Buyer Informed

One of the secrets to happy customers is to keep them informed (see below).

Pack It

All is for naught if the item arrives broken. Pack properly (page 122), and consider insurance (page 55).

Ship It

Choose the shipping option appropriate to the item and its destination (page 48), and consider using your computer to streamline the process (pages 124–127).

Keep in Touch

One of the secrets to happy customers is to keep them informed. Consider sending a quick email to your high bidder during each of these milestones.

When an auction closes. Include all the information we review on page 111.

When you receive payment. Thank the buyer and let him or her know you are leaving positive feedback, and when you expect the item to ship.

When you ship the item. Let the buyer know the shipment date, when the package should arrive, and any pertinent tracking information. Request that the buyer let you know when the item arrives safe and sound.

After shipping. Some buyers will remember to drop you a line when they receive their wares, but many forget or just don't bother. Inquire to see if the item has arrived in good condition. Encourage, but don't strong-arm, your buyers to leave positive feedback for you if they're happy with the transaction.

Getting Paid

What's the best part of an auction? Getting paid, of course. Whether your loot arrives digitally through PayPal or physically through the mail, there's something fun about getting money from a stranger. And if the money is for something that was just collecting dust in your attic, it's downright exhilarating.

But before you wallow in your cash, you have to receive it. When an auction ends, the next phase of your job begins. You need to communicate with your buyers to ensure that they pay promptly using one of the payment methods you specified when creating your auctions (see page 50).

Part of this communication involves sending an email invoice to your buyer. You can do this automatically through eBay, you can go the extra mile and send a personal email yourself, or both.

When all goes smoothly, your invoice will result in payment, either via the mail or through an online payment service. When that happens, it's time to leave positive feedback and then move on to the shipping room.

In the meantime, let's look at the process and politics behind getting paid.

Invoicing the eBay Way

When a successful auction ends, eBay jump-starts the communications process by immediately sending email to both the buyer and seller. The buyer receives an email congratulating him or her on winning the auction; this message contains payment details. If you've chosen to use eBay's Checkout option (see page 53) or you're using PayPal, this email will contain a button or link that will take the buyer through the checkout process.

As the seller, you'll receive an email containing your buyer's email address, as well as a link that lets you send an invoice through eBay's invoicing system. When you click this link, you'll be taken to the Send Invoice to Buyer page. (You can also get to this page by clicking the Send Invoice button that now appears on the listing page itself and in the Items I've Sold area of My eBay's All Selling page.)

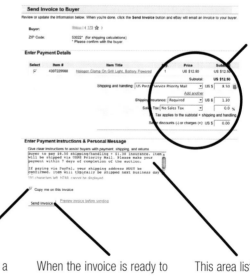

The shipping, insurance, and tax terms you specified when creating the auction appear here. If you aren't charging a flat rate for shipping, you can click on the calculator icon to calculate shipping costs (see page 51).

It's a good idea to receive a copy of the invoice so you know exactly what the buyer received.

When the invoice is ready to go, click Send Invoice.

This area lists the payment instructions that you typed when creating your auction. You can edit the text here as you see fit, or leave it as is.

Invoicing the Personal Way

It's great that eBay gets the ball rolling when an auction ends, and eBay's invoicing system is quick and convenient. But it's also impersonal. Rather than sending an invoice through eBay, we prefer to send our own email invoice to the winning bidder as soon as possible after an auction ends. This opens a personal line of communication that can be priceless should things go awry later.

As we mentioned, your high bidder's email address appears in the end-of-auction email that you receive from eBay. You can also set up your eBay preferences to have bidder email addresses appear in the listing page itself, as described on page 98.

What should your invoice email contain? Here's a sample.

Congratulations and thank you—you are the high bidder on the Palm V (8mb) w/2 cradles, plus more (item #194838960).

Your high bid was $74.66. Shipping will be $10.00, bringing your total to $84.66. I will be glad to insure the package for an additional $2.20. That would bring your total to $86.86.

You can pay via PayPal (gern@earthlink.net) or money order/cashier's check. You can mail the money order/cashier's check to:

Gern Blanston
PO Box 87365
Pittsburgh, PA 15222

Payment is due within 10 days of auction completion. Upon receipt of payment, I will ship your item via US Postal Service Priority Mail.

If you're paying via money order or cashier's check, please include a printout of this email along with your payment.

Please let me know what payment method you will be using and what your shipping address is so I can prepare your package.

Cheers and thanks again!

Gern Blanston

Start by thanking the buyer and reminding him or her what this email is about.

Restate the payment and shipping information included in your auction: payment options, shipping and insurance costs, and total amount due. If you didn't charge a flat fee for shipping, you'll need to calculate the final shipping cost. eBay's shipping calculator (see page 51) can help, as described below.

If you're accepting checks or money orders, be sure to include your mailing address.

Let the buyer know when you expect payment and how you will ship the item once you've been paid. Include any other specifics you mentioned in your auction, such as that items will be shipped after personal checks clear.

Ask your buyer to include a copy of your email with any form of mailed payment—it can be confusing to receive an envelope containing a lonely money order.

End the email by indicating what information you need from the buyer.

Calculating Shipping

If you included a shipping calculator in your listing, your end-of-auction email contains a Calculate Shipping link, as shown here. To calculate shipping, click the Calculate Shipping link and type the buyer's ZIP code (it's also in your end-of-auction email). The calculator displays the shipping costs, taking into account any handling charge you specified in the listing.

Payment details:
Item price:	US $15.65
Quantity:	1
Subtotal:	**US $15.65**
Shipping, handling:	Calculate Shipping
Shipping insurance per item:	
Sales tax:	(None)

Leaving Feedback: Critiquing Your Buyer

If you've already bought merchandise on eBay, you're probably familiar with feedback and its importance. Indeed, if you're a new seller, buying on eBay is a great way to establish a positive feedback profile. Start by being an exemplary buyer—buyers benefit from positive feedback, too (see page 23).

What is feedback? Think of it as eBay's version of the Better Business Bureau. Most eBay members deal with strangers. Feedback takes some of the mystery out of this equation—positive feedback ratings are reassuring, while a pattern of negatives is a red flag.

eBayers establish their reputations by accumulating feedback ratings. Your success on eBay—as a buyer or seller—can hinge on your positive feedback, or the lack thereof.

This brings us to the topic at hand. When an auction ends, you have 90 days to leave feedback for your buyer. But don't dawdle— we recommend leaving positive feedback as soon as you've received payment. (Assuming, of course, that your buyer has met your guidelines for payment amount, method, and timeliness.) Leaving feedback promptly helps establish good lines of communication and increases your chances of accumulating your own positive feedback.

eBay's feedback system protects its members from abuses. Only the winning bidder and seller can leave feedback for a specific auction. Of course, the content of that feedback is up to you.

Step 1.
Go to the Feedback Forum

To leave feedback, use eBay's Feedback Forum. You have several ways to get to the Feedback Forum; here are the methods we use most often.

Through My eBay's Items I've Sold List

In My eBay, go to the All Selling page, then use the Leave Feedback links in the Items I've Sold list.

If you don't see the Leave Feedback link, click the arrow and choose Leave Feedback from the drop-down menu.

Through the My eBay Feedback Page

If you have more than one review to write, use the My eBay Feedback page. To get there, click the Feedback link in the My eBay Views area. At the Feedback page, you can review auctions that are awaiting your feedback and see what folks have said about you lately.

When you click Leave Feedback, a page appears where you can write multiple reviews and submit them with a single click.

From the Item Page

If you sign in and then go to a completed auction's listing page, you'll find a Leave Feedback link.

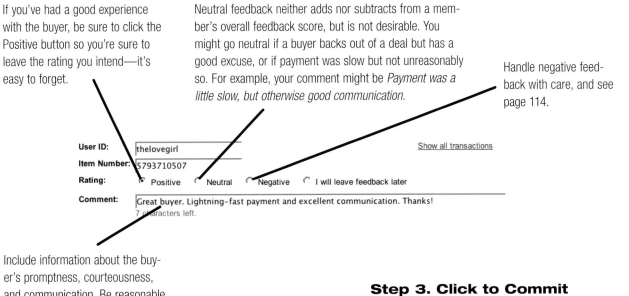

New Coach Signature cell phone case, gray/white NR

✓ The buyer has marked this item as "Payment Sent" on Aug-05-05.
Buyer's email:
Buyer's Postal Code: 9074

Print Shipping Label >

To print a US Postal Service or UPS shipping label online, click the **Print Shipping Label** button.

Other actions for this item:

You can manage all your items in My eBay and do the following:

- Mark payment received for this item.
- Mark the item shipped.
- Leave feedback for this item.
- View payment details.

Step 2. Write the Feedback

Now you're ready to review your buyer.

If you've had a good experience with the buyer, be sure to click the Positive button so you're sure to leave the rating you intend—it's easy to forget.

Neutral feedback neither adds nor subtracts from a member's overall feedback score, but is not desirable. You might go neutral if a buyer backs out of a deal but has a good excuse, or if payment was slow but not unreasonably so. For example, your comment might be *Payment was a little slow, but otherwise good communication.*

Handle negative feedback with care, and see page 114.

User ID:	thelovegirl	Show all transactions
Item Number:	5793710507	
Rating:	⊙ Positive ○ Neutral ○ Negative ○ I will leave feedback later	
Comment:	Great buyer. Lightning–fast payment and excellent communication. Thanks!	
	7 characters left.	

Include information about the buyer's promptness, courteousness, and communication. Be reasonable and honest. Avoid all-capital letters and lots of exclamation points—let your words do the talking.

Step 3. Click to Commit

Check your work once more, and when you're ready to commit, click the Leave Feedback button.

Going Negative

Negative feedback is serious business. It stains an eBay member's reputation, and as we've said again and again, reputation is everything on eBay.

Consider leaving negative comments only after you have exhausted all your options to resolve a conflict. Once you've left feedback, it's extremely difficult to retract—a truly unfortunate reality of eBay. What's more, eBay will never alter a comment and will consider removing comments only under very specific circumstances, such as if the feedback contains profane language.

Another reason to think twice before leaving negative feedback is that you may get negative feedback in return, especially if you acted hastily. One of your authors speaks from experience. In haste, Toby once left negative feedback for a seller she thought had never contacted her. Turns out he had sent an email that Toby's email program had misfiled. In response, he wrote the single piece of negative feedback in Toby's Member Profile. If she had given him the benefit of the doubt and looked a bit harder in her email folders, she'd have a perfect feedback rating.

We hope you never have to leave or respond to negative feedback. But if you do, here are some guidelines—and some tips that may help you avoid negatives the next time around.

Leaving Negative Feedback

If the time does come to leave negative feedback—perhaps a winning bidder simply fails to pay or contact you with any explanation—what should you write? Never use profanity, don't reveal personal identifying information about the buyer, and never be libelous or threatening.

Just state the facts—for example, *"Seller beware! This winning bidder never paid and never responded to my emails."*

When you submit a negative (or even neutral) feedback comment, eBay displays a last-chance screen that reminds you of the steps you can take to remedy a sour situation. eBay wants to make sure you've exhausted all options before going negative—you should, too.

I Beg to Differ: Responding to Feedback

If a buyer feels you have left unwarranted negative feedback or would like to offer an explanation, he or she can post a response. This feedback response will appear in his or her feedback forum under the original feedback left by you.

You have the same opportunity—you can respond to feedback left for you. In My eBay, go to the Feedback page. At the top of that page, click the Go to Feedback Forum link. Once at the Feedback Forum, click the Reply to Feedback Received link.

The page you are taken to contains all the feedback comments that have been left for you since you opened your account. Scroll down or click through the pages to find the feedback comment you would like to respond to. When you locate that feedback, click the Reply link. This takes you to the Reply to Feedback Received page.

All the same rules that apply to feedback comments (see page 113) also apply to responses. Don't make libelous or slanderous remarks. State the facts as you see them. You won't be able to retract your response.

Compose your response, review it once or twice to be sure you're not being too emotional, and click the Leave Reply button.

If you want to start from the beginning, click the Clear Form button.

Your response will appear beneath the original feedback comment for all to see. A response to a feedback comment is not reflected in your feedback rating, however.

It's simply an opportunity to tell your side of the story if you feel that there are extenuating circumstances or that the other party treated you unfairly.

A response appears below the original comment.

Comment	From	Date / Time	Item #
🔵 This winning bidder never paid and never responded to me. Seller beware!	Seller ▨▨▨▨ (231 ⭐)	Aug-07-05 12:20 ▨▨▨▨	
Reply by ▨▨▨▨ This was a misunderstanding. I sent responses to the wrong email address.		Aug-07-05 12:47	

The Feeling Is Mutual: Mutual Feedback Withdrawal

You reached the end of your rope and left negative feedback for a winning bidder. In retaliation, the winning bidder has left negative feedback for you, too. Everyone loses.

If you've resolved the disagreement with the other eBayer, there's still hope for reconciliation. You can't remove the negative feedback comment from your member profile or your bidder's, but you can initiate a process to repair the damage to your overall feedback rating. This process is called *Mutual Feedback Withdrawal*.

To begin, visit this page:

http://feedback.ebay.com/ws/eBayISAPI.dll?MFWRequest

Specify the item number for the listing and the message you would like to send to the buyer. After you click the Send Request button, the buyer will receive an email (and a message in his or her My Messages area) asking him or her to complete the process.

If he or she disagrees or doesn't respond in time (as described later), the feedback standing remains unchanged.

Once both you and the winning bidder have agreed to withdraw your feedback, eBay adjusts both of your feedback scores. Assuming you're removing negative feedback, your overall rating increases by one. eBay also posts a note next to the nega-

tive feedback comment stating that it has been withdrawn.

One-sided variations. If you haven't yet left feedback for the other eBayer and you go through the Mutual Feedback Withdrawal process, you won't be able to leave feedback for that particular transaction.

It works the other way, too: if the other eBayer hasn't left feedback for you and you withdraw a negative comment, he or she won't be able to leave feedback for you.

But wait: why would you go through Mutual Feedback Withdrawal when the feedback isn't yet mutual? Here's one example. Your buyer is slow to pay and never responds to your

correspondence. You leave appropriately scathing feedback. Then you hear from the buyer, who, as it turns out, was in the hospital. The buyer asks you to remove the negative feedback. Once you do so, the buyer can't leave feedback for that transaction.

This prohibition is intended to keep evil-minded eBayers from leaving negative feedback for members who have withdrawn theirs.

Timing. Mutual withdrawal of feedback must happen within 90 days of the end of the transaction or within 30 days of either party leaving feedback, whichever comes later.

Tips for a Happy Pay Day

A good way to avoid negative feedback is to make sure things don't go wrong in the latter stages of your auction—during that period after the auction ends but before the deal is completely done.

Here are some tips for a happy payday.

Write Early

As we mention on page 111, we're big fans of making the buying experience as personal as possible. If you leave the communication up to eBay, you don't develop a rapport with your buyer.

In this spirit, we encourage you to send a personal invoice as soon as an auction ends. Don't wait for hours or, perish the thought, days to pass. Let your buyer know right off the bat that you're on top of things and anxious to make sure the transaction goes as smoothly as possible.

Play the Waiting Game

If your buyer is a responsible eBayer, you should receive a response to your initial invoice email within a day or so. If your buyer responds with questions about shipping or payment options, respond quickly and courteously.

If you haven't heard back from the buyer after three days, it's time for a friendly reminder. We know you're anxious to wrap up your auction, but life happens and sometimes buyers need a little extra time.

Verify that you have your buyer's correct email address, and begin the subject of your reminder email with *REMINDER*. Politely remind your buyer that he or she was your high bidder, and include the date by which you expect payment. You can also send a reminder through My eBay's Selling tab, but it's much better to keep things personal and send an email yourself.

If we don't hear back within three days after sending the reminder, we typically send a final reminder that has a bit more of an urgent tone. The purpose of this email is to prompt the buyer to complete the transaction or, at least, be in touch with you. Begin the subject of this email with *FINAL REMINDER*.

If your buyer doesn't respond to this email promptly, it's time to start considering this auction a problem child. See page 136 for the next steps to take.

Don't Ship Until You're Paid

Regardless of the payment methods you accept, you should never ship an item until you've received payment. Wait until a cashier's check or money order arrives in the mail. As for personal checks, deposit them and wait until they clear. We know some eBay sellers accept personal checks and send items out before the checks clear, but we think doing so isn't worth the risk, particularly with pricey items.

Avoid Surprise Shipping Hikes

Once you learn your buyer's shipping address, you may find that the estimated shipping cost you listed in your auction is way off. If the actual shipping cost is lower than your estimation, let the buyer know he or she won't be paying as much as you originally estimated. Buyers love news like this.

And what if you underestimated your shipping costs? Take it on the chin and make up the difference yourself. This is not the time to tell your new friend that he or she will need to fork over more money.

Remember, one of the keys to a successful auction is to avoid surprises.

Confirm those Addresses

If you're accepting PayPal as one of your payment options, we recommend that you ask your buyers to use only a confirmed address. A confirmed address has been checked by PayPal against the billing address for the buyer's credit card. This is an important layer of fraud protection that you can add to your transaction.

But there's a problem. We often find that our PayPal buyers pay using an uncon-firmed address—even though our item descriptions clearly state that we require confirmed PayPal addresses.

There's a simple way to avoid this problem. By tweaking your PayPal preferences, you can choose to be informed when a buyer is trying to make payment with an uncon-firmed address.

Sign in to your PayPal account, and then click the Profile tab. Under Selling Preferences, click Payment Receiving Preferences. This preference area offers three choices.

We opt for the Ask Me preference, in which PayPal contacts you when a buyer without a confirmed address is attempting a payment. You can then contact the buyer with instructions on how to get his or her address confirmed, or suggest payment via another method that you accept. It's a more friendly way to approach the situation than simply refusing payment. And your buyer may well have a good reason why you should make an exception.

For more information about protecting yourself when using PayPal, see page 119.

Always block payments from US-based users without a confirmed address.

Always accept payments without a confirmed address.

Have PayPal contact you when a buyer without a confirmed address tries to pay.

PayPal®

Log Out | Help

| My Account | Send Money | Request Money | Merchant Tools | Auction Tools |

| Overview | Add Funds | Withdraw | History | Resolution Center | Profile |

Payment Receiving Preferences   Back to Profile Summary

Block payments from U.S. users who **do not** provide a Confirmed Address:
- ○ Yes
- ○ No
- ◉ Ask Me

Before You Ship

Your auction has ended and you've been paid. You've left positive feedback for your buyer, and now you're ready to fulfill your end of the deal by packing and shipping your item to its new owner.

Before you do, take a breath—you have a few things to think about before you ship. Is the buyer's address legitimate? How can you be sure? Is the item really ready to go to a complete stranger, or does some personal information appear somewhere on it or its box?

The moment that a package leaves your hands, you lose the opportunity to double-check critical details like these. This is the "an ounce of prevention is worth a pound of cure" phase of your auction. Here's your ounce.

Too Much Information

Reusing old shipping boxes? Packing an electronics item in its original box? Good for you. But remember to scan the inside of each box thoroughly and be certain that you aren't sending any personal or sensitive information to your buyer —an address, phone number, or credit card number that you might not want to share.

Remove any old receipts and communications from inside the box. Check the exterior of all boxes for receipts or packing slips that might be tucked into plastic pockets. And while you're at it, use a black pen to thoroughly cross out any old barcodes that could cause problems with your shipper.

Selling Computers? Clean the Slate

If you're selling a used computer system, be sure to thoroughly erase its hard drive. (We'll explain what we mean by *thoroughly* in a moment.)

That sounds like an obvious step, but you'd be surprised at how many people omit it or don't do it properly. In a recent study conducted by a data-recovery firm, over seventy percent of hard drives bought on eBay contained sensitive personal or business data. The firm bought 200 drives and was able to recover 3.3 million files, including 40,000 Microsoft Word documents, 15,000 Excel spreadsheets, and about 50 complete email inboxes.

We found this study data to be interesting and slightly terrifying. The moral? When selling used computers, be sure to securely reformat every single drive before you ship. That means more than simply deleting files from the hard drive—you need to use an application that will overwrite *all* the data on the drive. For Windows, you can use utilities such as Detto Technologies' SecureClean (www.detto.com) or Symantec's Norton Utilities (www.symantec.com). For the Mac, consider Micromat's TechTool Deluxe (www.micromat.com).

This tip also applies to other electronic devices, such as iPods, personal digital assistants, and cell phones. Erase before you ship.

Seeking Delivery Confirmation

It has happened to us. A well-packed item sets out on its journey to a new home, never to arrive.

There's an easy way to confirm that a package finds its new home: use your shipper's *Delivery Confirmation* service. As we describe later in this chapter, if you're shipping through the US Postal Service, Delivery Confirmation is a great way to track your shipment if your buyer claims it never arrived. USPS Delivery Confirmation service is cheap, and if you purchasing postage online, it's free (see page 127). All shipments sent via FedEx and UPS have tracking service included.

Protection by PayPal: Seller Protection Policy

PayPal's Seller Protection Policy (SPP) can help prevent you from getting stung by false claims and no-good buyers. But you have to play by PayPal's rules; for a transaction to be SPP-eligible, it must meet the following criteria:

- You must have a Verified Business or Premier Account.

- Your buyer must have a confirmed address (see page 117), and you must ship to that address. The confirmed address appears on the Transaction Details page.

- If the item is worth $250 or more, you must require a signed receipt upon delivery.

- You must be able to produce proof of postage that can be tracked online.

Sellers in the US, UK, and Canada are eligible to receive up to $5,000 in annual coverage. For more information about the Seller Protection Policy, visit the PayPal Help area by going to www.paypal.com and clicking the Help link at the top of the page.

Cross-Check Shipping Addresses

If you choose to allow a buyer to pay through PayPal and you don't require him or her to have a confirmed address, at least

check to be sure that the buyer's eBay account is registered in the same country to which you are shipping the item. Disparate shipping and registration information can often be a red flag for a potential scam. Check the buyer's member profile to confirm that this information matches.

Pixel Trail: Save Your Email

One of the best ways to follow the trail of an eBay transaction is to be able to refer back to all communications you've had with a seller. We find it extremely helpful to keep a folder where we keep all follow-up communications with buyers. We tend to keep these messages for at least a year, just in case. That old correspondence uses hardly any disc space, and it can be a tremendous help in sorting out a misunderstanding—or in backing up a claim.

Verify that Escrow Service

We're hearing more and more stories about fake escrow sites being set up to take the money and run. If you and your buyer have agreed to use a third-party escrow service, do your homework and verify that the company exists. Look the company's number up in the phone book and give it a call. Be certain that the company is bonded. Companies bonded in the US have a license you can request to see.

Packing and Shipping at a Glance

True story: The brother of one of your co-authors once had a part-time job for a major shipping company that shall remain nameless. On his first day, said brother was getting a tour of the shipping warehouse from a grizzled foreman. At one point, the foreman picked up a box marked *fragile*. "See this word?" he asked, "It don't mean squat!" And with that, he hurled the box into a brown truck with such force that the box began making a rattling sound that it wasn't making before.

We have no doubt that most of the people who load brown trucks—and indeed, trucks of all colors—do so with care and respect for the cargo they carry. And yet the worst does happen, and you must prepare for it. It's your package versus the world, so pack defensively.

Before you send your package into the world, you'll want to do some planning. If your item is heavy or oversized, for example, you may need to use a freight service or arrange for the buyer to pick it up (see page 128). And you'll need to address the mundane chores behind creating shipping labels. Yes, you can scrawl addresses by hand, but we have some techniques that are easier and more accurate (see pages 124–127).

Packing and shipping aren't exactly glamorous activities, but they're critical phases of the online auction process—if your item arrives broken, you're looking at refunding your buyer's money, making an insurance claim, and possibly receiving negative feedback. Those are adventures worth avoiding.

Outfitting Your Shipping Room

Here's a checklist of the items you'll want for your packing and shipping endeavors.

Boxes and containers. eBay sellers tend to develop an unusual passion for cardboard. If the box containing your latest mail-order purchase seems as exciting as the purchase itself, you know you've arrived as a seller.

Boxes come in all shapes and sizes, but they should all meet certain criteria. Be sure they're made of sturdy, corrugated cardboard. If you're recycling a box from your latest Victoria's Secret order, be sure there are no weak spots that could collapse under pressure, and that all the flaps are intact.

If you're shipping electronics, cameras, or computer gear, use the original boxes (if you still have them). Chances are that they contain specially fitted pieces of foam designed by engineers whose job is to thwart grizzled shipping foremen. (And no matter what you're selling, it's always a plus to include the original packaging and a mention of it in your item description, as noted on page 85.) Even if the original packaging isn't quite sturdy enough to go it alone, it will make a fine starting point.

There's a whole galaxy of specialized boxes and padded envelopes: CD and DVD mailers, videotape boxes, cassette mailers, cardboard tubes, and more. On the opposite page, we've listed some sources for these and other packing materials.

Bubble wrap. Most items can benefit from being snuggled in at least one layer of bubble wrap. Wrapping small things in bubble wrap also helps prevent them from getting lost in a larger box. You don't want your buyer to accidentally throw away any small accessories that accompany your item.

Packing peanuts. When boxing something, it's a good idea to fill the extra space around your item with packing material. Packing peanuts—those tumbleweeds of the modern age—are clean and lightweight. You can buy them, but chances are you receive your share of them in your own purchases. So do the Earth and your wallet a favor and reuse your peanuts.

Peanuts can be made of either Styrofoam or biodegradable vegetable starch. How can you tell what kind you have? Dip one peanut in water. If it dissolves, it's made of starch and thus won't become a permanent resident of a landfill. If you're including foam peanuts in your packaging, consider including recycling information in the box (see page 134).

Tip: If you're shipping electronics, avoid Styrofoam peanuts or newspaper—they can generate a static charge that can damage sensitive electronics. Use starch peanuts or buy anti-static peanuts.

Newspaper. It's free, it provides good shock absorption, it's easily recyclable, and it's messy. If you're using newspaper for fill, wrap your item in a plastic bag or bubble wrap so that it doesn't come in contact with the newsprint. Either crumple up the paper loosely or buy an inexpensive shredder and shred away. We find that shredding makes the paper a little less unwieldy. We shred as we go, since shredded paper takes up more space than its intact counterpart.

Tape. Packing tape comes in several flavors: strapping tape, sealing tape, water-activated kraft paper tape, industrial tape—you get the idea. Take your pick, but be sure to use tape made for packaging. Don't use masking tape or cellophane tape.

We use clear tape for sealing bubble wrap, taping over address labels to keep them protected, and sealing smaller packages such as envelopes. To seal heavy boxes, we use strapping tape, which is reinforced with glass or nylon filaments. If you plan to sell more than a few items, buy a tape gun to make dispensing easy. You can then buy inexpensive refills.

The Rest. Other items for your shipping shopping list include a box cutter or X-Acto knife, cardboard for stiffening envelopes and protecting photos and magazines, disposable diapers for items with breakable appendages (see page 135), plastic bags for keeping items clean and dry, black permanent markers (we love Sharpies), shipping labels (see pages 124–127), tissue paper, an inexpensive postal scale, and scissors.

Where to Find Supplies

There's no place like home. Save sturdy, undamaged boxes and the bubble wrap and fill that comes with them. Peel or cut off any existing labels or cover them with brown packing tape.

If you strike out at home, look around town. Chances are local retailers have plenty of used materials that they'd otherwise have to pay to get rid of.

Many shippers, including FedEx, UPS, and Airborne Express, provide free boxes and supplies.

The US Postal Service offers free boxes, tubes, labels, and envelopes. Your local post office probably has some of these items, and you can order the whole line in larger quantities at http://supplies.usps.gov. Note that the supplies are stamped with various Postal Service delivery options, such as Express Mail and Priority Mail. Order supplies in accordance with the shipping method you plan to use; for example, don't order Priority Mail boxes unless you're planning to use Priority Mail service.

If you're looking to buy supplies in bulk, check out eBay. Search for specific supplies, or browse the following category:

Business & Industrial > Office, Printing & Shipping > Shipping & Packing Supplies

Of course, you can also buy shipping supplies at a local retailer or order them online from suppliers such as www.papermart.com and www.fast-pack.com.

Keep it Clean

No one wants to open a box and be greeted by a cloud of dust and cat hair. Keep your packing materials clean and avoid scrounging up stained and dusty boxes and peanuts. If you're saving packing peanuts or shredded paper, store them in plastic bags, away from pet hair and dust. If someone in your household smokes, consider keeping your supplies in a smoke-free room or somewhere outside the house. The smell of smoke can linger and make for an unhappy buyer.

Packing Your Shipment

Packing a box—brain surgery, right? Of course not. And yet this is one of those steps that can make or literally break an auction.

Here's a step-by-step packing guide. The following instructions assume that you're using a box to ship your item. For more packing tips and advice on using specialized shipping containers, such as media mailers or tubes, see page 133.

Step 1. Select the right box.

Choose a box that's approximately 25 to 30 percent larger than the item you're shipping. This allows for plenty of room for shock-absorbing fill. But don't go too far—if the box is too big, you'll waste packing materials and will end up paying too much for shipping. As a general rule, keep two or three inches of protection around your item.

Tip: If your item is particularly fragile or valuable, you might want to double-box it to provide more protection. Pack the item as described here, then tuck its box into a second box that's a few inches larger on all sides. Surround the inner box with packing material as described below.

Step 2. Prepare the item.

Place a layer of peanuts, newspaper, or other fill on the bottom of the box. Center the wrapped item on top of the fill. The object of the game is to keep your item as close to the center of the box as possible so that it's safe from external trauma. If the item has several pieces, be sure to place fill between the pieces so they don't bang against each other during shipping. If things look tight, get a larger box.

Most items can benefit from being wrapped in bubble wrap or foam. This will help keep your item clean and dry and will provide extra protection against shock. If you're shipping a fragile item that has more than one part—such as the antique sugar bowl and lid shown here—wrap each part separately.

It's easy for small parts to get lost in the peanuts. A brightly colored adhesive dot helps each part get noticed.

Tips

If you're shipping a book or other flat document, place the item inside a plastic bag or wrap it in plastic wrap.

If the item has breakable appendages, be sure not to wrap it too tightly. The wrap itself can exert too much pressure and cause a break. Take it easy when taping bubble wrap around an item. It's frustrating to do surgery on an item to free it from its wrapping, and your buyer might break something in the struggle.

Step 3. Bring in Doctor Fill.

Fill the remaining empty space with packing material. If you're using peanuts, be sure to pack them tightly—they tend to settle in transit. The fill should come up to the top seam of the box, but should not make the flaps awkward to close. Close the flaps (don't tape them yet), and give the box a good shake. If you hear your item shifting around, add more fill.

If you're including a packing list, a "thank you" note, or any other paperwork in your package (see page 132), place it below the top layer of fill. If you place it on the very top, your buyer may accidentally slice through it when opening the box.

Tip: It takes a lot of newspaper to fill big spaces properly, and in a large package, all that paper adds up to additional weight and shipping costs. We hate storing peanuts, too, but the fact is, they're the most economical packing material where shipping costs are concerned.

Step 4. Secure the box.

Close the flaps and tape the box closed.

Remove any old labels and shipping stickers, which can confuse a shipper, particularly if the stickers contain barcodes that might be scanned by mistake.

Avoid placing labels on a seam or on top of the packing tape used to seal the box. If the tape comes loose, your box may never find its way. If you've printed a plain-paper or peel-and-stick label, put strips of wide, clear packing tape over the label to keep it from smearing or coming loose. Don't tape over a barcode, though.

If you're using strapping tape, two or three strips across the center seam of the top flaps should do. If you're using paper tape or non-reinforced packing tape, put three or four strips down the center, then add a strip down each side for good measure.

Recycling a box? Reinforce its corners and bottom seam with some strapping tape.

Step 5. Attach the label.

Attach the label to the top of the box. The "top" doesn't necessarily have to be the side that opens. If the box is more stable on its side, then put it on its side and affix the label to the panel that's facing up. If you're using a shipping label and pouch, follow the carrier's instructions for applying the label.

If you're using courier air bills that tuck inside a plastic pouch, consider also writing the recipient's address directly on the box. If the air bill is lost, the package will still have an address on it.

For advice on creating labels, see the following pages.

Shipping the eBay Way

As we mentioned in Chapter 2, eBay and its PayPal subsidiary work hand-in-hand with the Postal Service and UPS. If you use PayPal, eBay makes it a breeze to manage the mechanics of purchasing postage, and printing shipping labels for the US Postal Service or UPS.

When an auction is completed and you've received payment, just head to My eBay. From there, you can choose your preferred shipper, pay for shipping, and print a shipping label. eBay supplies the buyer's shipping address for you and charges the shipping costs to your PayPal account.

It's all so easy, why *wouldn't* you ship the eBay way? Maybe you don't use PayPal. Maybe you're shipping via FedEx or a trucking company. Or maybe you just don't have access to a printer when it comes time to ship.

But if you're like us, you'll find the eBay/PayPal approach to shipping makes the process very convenient.

Set Up for Shipping

Step 1. Go to My eBay, locate the item you're about to ship, and click the Print Shipping Label link in the Action drop-down menu. When asked, sign in to PayPal.

> Print Shipping Label ⌄

Tip: Need to ship several items? Click the check box next to each item, then click the Print Shipping Labels button below the Items I've Sold list.

Step 2. Double-check the address information at the top of the page (see opposite page). To change any address information, use the Edit this Address link.

Step 3. Choose shipment and insurance options as described at right. (If you're using UPS, the options will look a bit different. For background on the services the Postal Service and UPS provide, see page 48.)

Step 4. Check your work, then click the Continue button near the bottom of the page. Review the confirmation page that appears, using its links to fix any problems. Then, click the Pay and Continue button.

Step 5. Print your label. A window opens showing a sample of the label you're about to print. Once you've successfully printed your label, click the OK button. For a look at a sample label and some peel-and-stick paper recommendations, see page 126.

Tips

Reprint or refund? If you need to void the label or reprint it, use the History tab of your My Account screen on PayPal. You have 48 hours to void a label for a package you haven't shipped.

Track it. You can also track a package from the History tab of your My Account screen. Or, use My eBay: locate the listing in the Items I've Sold area, open the Action drop-down menu for the auction, and click View Shipment Status.

This buyer doesn't have a confirmed address. To be protected by PayPal you are required to ship to a confirmed address; see page 119.

Choose the service on which you and the buyer have agreed. If your auction listing stated that you'd use a specific service—for example, Priority Mail—make good on your promise.

Want to create a UPS label instead? Click here to change shippers.

Make this choice based on the size of the package and the packaging you're using.

Choose the date you plan to mail the package. Accuracy counts: the post office can refuse packages that don't have the correct mailing date.

If you used the shipping calculator, eBay supplies the weight for you. **Tip:** When weighing your item, always round up to the next pound.

Delivery Confirmation service is always free when buying postage online from the US Postal Service.

PayPal sends your buyer an email when you purchase postage for the item. This is the spot to craft any messages you might want to place in that email.

If purchasing insurance from the US Postal Service, the maximum declared value is limited to $200. Need to insure for more? Head for the post office.

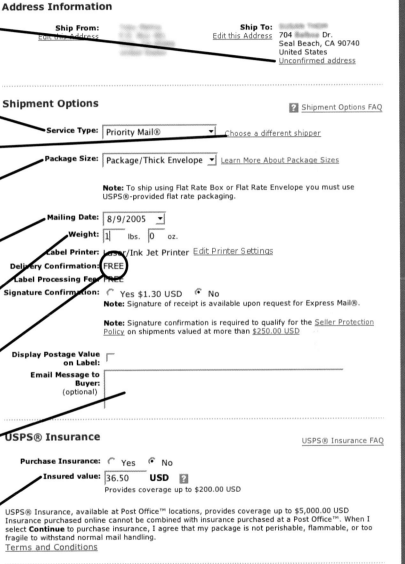

Address Information

Ship From:
Edit this Address

Ship To:
Edit this Address   704 ___ Dr.
Seal Beach, CA 90740
United States
Unconfirmed address

Shipment Options   ? Shipment Options FAQ

Service Type: Priority Mail®   ▼   Choose a different shipper

Package Size: Package/Thick Envelope ▼ Learn More About Package Sizes

Note: To ship using Flat Rate Box or Flat Rate Envelope you must use USPS®-provided flat rate packaging.

Mailing Date: 8/9/2005 ▼
Weight: 1 lbs. 0 oz.
Label Printer: Laser/Ink Jet Printer Edit Printer Settings
Delivery Confirmation: FREE
Label Processing Fee: FREE
Signature Confirmation: ○ Yes $1.30 USD ⊙ No
Note: Signature of receipt is available upon request for Express Mail®.

Note: Signature confirmation is required to qualify for the Seller Protection Policy on shipments valued at more than $250.00 USD

Display Postage Value on Label: ☐
Email Message to Buyer: (optional)

USPS® Insurance   USPS® Insurance FAQ

Purchase Insurance: ○ Yes ⊙ No
Insured value: 36.50 **USD** ?
Provides coverage up to $200.00 USD

USPS® Insurance, available at Post Office™ locations, provides coverage up to $5,000.00 USD Insurance purchased online cannot be combined with insurance purchased at a Post Office™. When I select **Continue** to purchase insurance, I agree that my package is not perishable, flammable, or too fragile to withstand normal mail handling.
Terms and Conditions

Item(s) Being Shipped to Your Buyer

Note: If you have multiple packages for this transaction, you can print multiple labels by clicking the **Ship multiple boxes for this order** link after creating the current label.

Item #	Item Title	Qty
6789930350	New Coach Signature cell phone case, gray/white NR	1

More Ways to Create Shipping Labels

A package without a shipping label isn't going anywhere. As we showed on the previous pages, if you ship the eBay way—taking advantage of eBay's tie-ins with PayPal to pay for shipping—you can print US Postal Service or UPS shipping labels as part of the process.

If you don't want to use PayPal or you'd just like to investigate your other labeling options, read on. You have other options for putting addresses on paper.

And do you have to use your computer to address outgoing packages? No. But using your computer offers some big advantages. First of all, its writing may be neater than yours. Another advantage is accuracy. You can copy your buyer's address from an eBay email or other correspondence, and then paste it into whatever program you use to create labels. Copying and pasting the address eliminates the risk of making a mistake that could delay your shipment—or worse.

Finally, creating shipping labels can save you money and may even help your package get to its destination a bit faster. If you create a label using your chosen carrier's Web site (or through eBay and PayPal, as described on the previous pages), the label will contain bar codes and other information that the carrier's automated scanning equipment can use. Because carriers like it when you play by their rules, they'll often throw in additional services, such as delivery confirmation.

Option 1:
Your Word Processor or Other Software

Here's the quickest way to create a label: copy your buyer's name and address from your end-of-auction eBay email or other correspondence, and then paste it into your word processor. Use your word processor's formatting commands to make the recipient's name and address big and bold. The US Postal Service says the address should be "legible from an arm's length away," presumably to accommodate postal workers who forget their reading glasses.

Next, print out the page, cut out the address, and use wide, clear shipping tape to attach it to your parcel. Write your return address on the parcel or attach one of those return-address stickers that your favorite charity sent you, securing it with a piece of tape, too.

Make a template. To take this approach one step further, use your word processor to create a label template that also contains your return address.

If you're using Microsoft Word, position both addresses within a two-column, two-row table. Resize the columns as shown here to bump the recipient's address to the right. Finally, turn off the table's borders and shading to avoid printing those lines on your label.

When you need a label, open this template, replace the recipient's address, and print. If you often create several labels at a time, copy and paste the template so it appears a few times on one sheet of paper.

Get templates online. Avery (www.avery.com) sells a stationery closet's worth of pre-cut, peel-and-stick shipping labels. At Avery's Web site, you can visit the Blank Template Library and download free Microsoft Word templates that are already formatted for a variety of label sizes. Simply open the template that matches your label stock, add your return address and recipient's address, and print.

Option 2:
Your Shipper's Web Site

Each major shipper's Web site has services for creating shipping labels.

US Postal Service. You can create labels with or without postage using the Postal Service's Click-N-Ship site (sss-web.usps.com). Register for a free USPS account, and you can create a Priority Mail or Express Mail address label, complete with postage, which is charged to your credit card. (If you aren't using USPS flat-rate packaging, you'll need a postal scale—we got ours on eBay for under $30.)

Printing postage-paid labels can save you some post office waiting time. If the package weighs less than one pound, you can drop it in a mailbox—no standing in line. (Packages that weigh more must be handed to a letter carrier or post office employee.) This is so speedy and convenient that we now create postage-paid labels for every package we mail, whether it's an eBay sale or not.

If you don't have a postal scale or you don't want to create a USPS account, you can still use this site to create labels without postage.

Mac users: At this writing, Mac users must use the Firefox browser to produce labels; Apple's Safari doesn't work. (Download Firefox at www.getfirefox.com.) With Firefox, a PDF of your label is downloaded to your computer. You can print that PDF using Adobe Acrobat. (Download the free Acrobat Reader at www.acrobat.com.)

The USPS site "standardizes" addresses to conform to postal regulations and automation requirements. Also note the lack of commas and periods in addresses—the post office recommends against them. (Keep that in mind next time you're addressing holiday cards.)

As mentioned on page 125, the USPS gives you free delivery confirmation service when you purchase postage online.

Never put tape over a barcode; it could cause scanning problems.

Tip: If you print a lot of USPS labels, check out the peel-and-stick labels from Label Universe (www.labeluniverse.com). They're designed specifically for the Click-N-Ship label format.

UPS and FedEx. If you've registered for a free UPS or FedEx account, you can create pre-paid shipping labels online. Take the labeled package to a UPS or FedEx drop-box or retail location, and you'll avoid a pickup charge. Unlike the USPS, both UPS and FedEx will bill you for your shipping charges.

Need a refund? If you printed a label you don't need, the USPS gives you ten days to request a refund. Log into your Click-N-Ship account and click the Shipping History link. When your shipping history appears, locate the label for which you want a refund and click its number. In the Label Details screen that appears next, click Request Refund.

Another way to request a refund is to go to your USPS Click-N-Ship My Account page and click the Request a Refund link. A new screen appears where you type the transaction and label numbers. (They're on the label itself and in the confirmation email you received when you originally created the label.)

No matter which technique you use, don't hold your breath waiting for your refund. The Postal Service says you should allow up to two credit card billing cycles for your refund to post. To check the status of the refund, use the Shipping History feature of the Click-N-Ship site.

Bigger Than a Breadbox: Shipping Large Items

eBay is about more than collectibles, clothes, and electronics. People buy and sell big stuff, too—car engines, water heaters, industrial compressors. (We once listed a massive, commercial-grade cigar humidor, although it didn't receive any bids. Imagine that.)

Unless you're willing to have your buyer pick them up in person, super-sized items must be shipped via a freight or trucking company. Dealing with these companies isn't the same as dealing with the Postal Service, UPS, or FedEx. The packing requirements, costs, and shipping policies are different. And the trucks are bigger.

If you're like us and you sell mostly small stuff, you don't have to deal with the joy of crating and the glamour of loading docks. But if you plan to sell big stuff, read on for an overview of the issues involved in getting it from here to there. In fact, it's a good idea to familiarize yourself with freight issues before listing a large or heavy item, since you'll want to include shipping information in the item listing.

Finally, it is worth remembering that you don't have to ship big items if you don't want to. If you opt for local pickup only when specifying your shipping policies (see page 50), your buyer is responsible for picking up the item. Requiring local pickup may simplify your life, but it significantly reduces the pool of likely bidders. If you take this route, be sure your item description and payment instructions make it clear that you don't do shipping.

Does It Need to Go Freight?

The Postal Service, UPS, and FedEx each have maximum size and weight limits. The weight limits are easy to understand, but the size limits are trickier than you might think. To determine your package's size, you need to do a little math.

Step 1. Measure the object's longest side—this is its length.

Step 2. Measure the object's girth—the distance all the way around the package at its widest point, perpendicular to the length.

Step 3. Add the girth and the length to arrive at the package size. For example, if the girth is 70 inches and the length is 40 inches, the package size is 110 inches.

US Postal Service. A package can't weigh more than 70 pounds, regardless of the mail service you choose. For Priority Mail and Express Mail shipments, the package size must not exceed 108 inches. Packages sent via Parcel Post—which we like to call "slow boat"—can measure up to 130 inches, although surcharges apply for packages over 35 pounds (25 pounds for books and paper matter).

FedEx. For FedEx Home Delivery packages, the weight limit is 70 pounds. For FedEx Ground packages, the weight limit is 150 pounds. The size limit for both is 165 inches, and maximum length is 108 inches. For FedEx Express service, the weight limit is 150 pounds. Maximum size is 165 inches with a maximum length of 119 inches.

UPS. Maximum weight is 150 pounds, but packages weighing more than 70 pounds require a special heavy-package label. Maximum size is 165 inches, and maximum length is 108 inches.

Shipping via Freight

You've made the measurements and determined that your item needs to be shipped as freight through a trucking company. Now you need to decide which carrier to use, what type of service you want, and whether you'll do the packaging or have someone else do it for you. Each of these decisions will affect shipping costs, and you'll want to give your bidders as much information as possible early on.

A great place to go for help with these decisions is eBay's Freight Resource Center, which is a joint venture between eBay and Freightquote.com (http://ebay. freightquote.com). With the Freight Resource Center, you can choose a shipping method, get rate information, create a freight calculator for your listing page, track shipments, and print the official bill of lading documents that your carrier requires. When your auction closes, you can use the Freight Resource Center to schedule your shipment.

Want to look for a freight company on your own? Check out our list of suggestions on page 135.

Shipping Criteria

Whether or not you use the Freight Resource Center, you'll need to provide a lot of information in order to get an accurate estimate of shipping costs. Be prepared to answer the following questions.

What's inside? You'll need to identify what you're shipping. Be as accurate as possible.

How many? Does your shipment include one item or several? A dining table with four chairs is five items. On the other hand, four boxes of tile that have the identical size and weight are considered a single item.

Is it packed? If you want someone else to do the packing for you, just say so. And be prepared to pay for it.

How big and how heavy? You'll need to provide the dimensions and weight of your shipment. The shipper may verify your declared weight; if you've greatly underestimated it, your charges will be higher than your estimate. Remember, weight includes any packaging.

Where oh where? Be prepared to provide ZIP codes for the pickup and delivery locations. (If you're creating a freight calculator, you don't have to specify a delivery ZIP code.) Other location-oriented details can also affect pricing and choice of carrier: Are the locations residences? Is there a loading dock? Will the driver need to go inside?

If you're using the Freight Resource Center, you supply this information in a series of screens. Once you've done that, a screen appears containing the lowest price quote from the Freightquote database of shippers.

Results

Carrier: **NORTH AMERICAN VAN LINES**
Origin: **95466 - Philo, CA**
Destination: **90035 - Los Angeles, CA**

Transit time:	10 business days	(Click to apply service)
Shipping cost:	$441.76	
Insurance:	$44.00	☐
NON-COMMERCIAL PICKUP	$53.00	
LIFTGATE PICKUP	$0.00	
NON-COMMERCIAL DELIVERY	$53.00	
ARRIVAL NOTIFICATION	$0.00	
LIFTGATE DELIVERY	$0.00	
FUEL SURCHARGE*	$81.03	
Total:	$628.79	Recalculate Total

Shipping cost is listed in US Dollars
Carrier liability is limited to their determination of "fair value," which in no case can exceed $45.00 (US Dollars)

Continue ▶

If you choose to add the freight calculator, it appears at the bottom of your auction listing, allowing potential bidders to plug in their ZIP codes and other details to get a shipping estimate.

Freight Shipping Calculator

Please Select the Destination:
- ⦿ US/Canada, enter zip code 98101
- ◯ International

Calculate

When your auction containing the freight calculator has closed, you can go to the Freight Resource Center's Ship It tab to schedule your shipment.

Going Global: International Shipping

If you're reading this, you've either decided to ship internationally or you're pondering doing so. As we've said previously, being willing to ship outside the US increases your potential bidder pool, but requires research and effort.

The most critical factor deals with the legalities of international shipping. Every country has a Byzantine set of prohibitions, restrictions, and requirements for incoming shipments, and if you ignore them, your carefully packed item could be refused by the local customs office.

Some restrictions, such as those banning shipments of firearms and human remains, are obvious. But many restrictions are mysterious and rooted in cultural obscurities and protectionist trade laws. For example, you can't legally mail a phonograph to Argentina or "horror comics" to Great Britain. And don't even think about mailing a clock or a bell to Italy.

You also need to take customs regulations into account. Some countries impose duty fees and taxes for incoming packages. Generally, you'll be passing those costs on to your buyer, and if you use the US Postal Service, that means figuring the costs out in advance. (UPS and FedEx build these costs into your shipping fee.)

Then there's packing. You may want to add some extra fill and bubble wrap to ensure that your item will withstand its voyage. If something breaks in transit, resolving problems can be complicated by language barriers, time differences, and currency-conversion issues.

Is it Legal?

First things first: determine whether your item can legally be shipped to a specific country.

A great resource for determining what you can ship to a given country is the US Postal Service's International Rate Calculator (http://ircalc.usps.gov). Click the Complete International Rate Charts link. In the screen that appears next, click the name of the desired country. In the *next* screen, you'll see Prohibitions, Restrictions, Observations, and rate information.

Another site to bookmark is FedEx's Global Trade Manager site (www.fedex.com/us/international), where you can read country-by-country profiles and restrictions, download shipping documents, and much more.

Check and double-check the specifics of shipping to a particular country. Besides a duty fee, a buyer may have to pay a tax or an administrative fee for customs clearance. Let buyers know what to expect so they aren't surprised when they have to fork over more dough to get their packages. For instance, USPS Global Express Mail packages to Great Britain can cost the recipient upwards of $15 in acceptance fees.

An international package must go through a customs broker in order to be allowed into another country. All major shippers provide brokerage as part of their service, but filling out the paperwork is still up to you. The specific forms you need to complete depend on which shipper you use.

Tip: eBay's Global Trade center (http://pages.ebay.com/globaltrade) is a fine resource for sellers contemplating going global.

Choosing a Shipper

Here's an overview of the most useful international shipping services provided by the US Postal Service, UPS, and FedEx.

US Postal Service. Most international sellers recommend using the US Postal Service for shipping, and we heartily agree. The USPS tends to have the lowest rates and has a large selection of service options.

Global Priority Mail is an excellent option for parcels weighing four pounds or less. Delivery typically takes four to six days and service is available to over 51 countries. Rates start at $4 and vary depending on destination and weight of your package. Flat-rate envelopes are available for $5 and $9 ($4 and $7 to Canada and Mexico). Return receipt, recorded delivery, and insurance services are not available with Global Priority Mail.

Global Express Mail comes with a bigger sticker price but provides faster delivery and more amenities. Average delivery time is three to five days and service is available to over 175 countries. Tracking and return-receipt services are available for some destinations. You can create and print shipping labels online and pay for postage as well. Weight limits range from 22 pounds to 70 pounds, depending on the destination. Although these packages supposedly receive priority handling, you won't get your money back if they aren't delivered within the estimated timeframe. Shipping fees include $100 insurance, and you can buy up to $5,000 worth of additional coverage.

Global Airmail service is available in two flavors: as letter-post (four pounds or less) or Parcel Post (maximum weight of 45 to 70 pounds, depending on destination). Both services are often less expensive than Global Priority Mail, but delivery times can be a bit slower: four to seven days for letter-post and four to ten days for Parcel Post. Return receipt service is available for both letter-post and Parcel Post; insurance is available for Parcel Post only.

Global Economy service is also available as letter-post or Parcel Post, with the same weight limitations. Global Economy is often half the price of Global Airmail, but it's slow. Global Economy packages typically travel by *surface mail*—ship or truck—no first-class seats for these packages. The postal service claims delivery times of four to six weeks, but ten weeks isn't unusual.

To learn more about USPS international shipping, ask your local postmaster or visit www.usps.com/global.

UPS. UPS's services are fast, reasonably priced, and provide all-inclusive rates, including customs clearance. Free pickup—and three free delivery attempts—make UPS a fine alternative to the Postal Service.

UPS Worldwide Expedited is our service of choice when shipping internationally with UPS. UPS guarantees on-time delivery of your package to more than 52 countries. A brown truck will even pick up your package for free. As with all UPS shipments, $100

of insurance is included in the shipping price. Deliveries to Mexico and Canada are guaranteed to arrive at most destinations within three business days. Deliveries to Asia and Europe are guaranteed to arrive at most destinations within four to five business days.

UPS builds customs-clearance fees into your shipping price, which helps avoid extra-charge surprises when the package arrives at its destination.

You can learn more about this and other UPS international shipping services at www.ups.com.

FedEx. Like UPS, FedEx provides door-to-door service and customs-cleared delivery to major locations worldwide. FedEx service is available to more countries than UPS World Expedited service. If you need to put a little extra zip into your package delivery, FedEx is a good choice.

FedEx Express International Economy service provides a good combination of speed and cost efficiency. Express International Economy service is available to more than 210 countries. Delivery usually takes two to three business days to Mexico, Canada, and Puerto Rico, and two to five days elsewhere.

To explore FedEx's international service options, visit FedEx's Global Trade Manager site at the address provided on the opposite page.

Shipping and Packing Tips

Batteries Included

It's always nice for buyers to find a little something in their packages that they weren't expecting. If an item you sold needs batteries, consider including a fresh set. Wrap them well, and don't bury them among packing peanuts where they may be missed.

Other items you might want to add to the box include the following.

A packing list. Let a buyer know how many items he or she should be fishing out of the box so that nothing gets thrown out. On this printout, include the shipping address in large, bold letters. If the external label falls off during shipping, anyone opening the package will know where it was headed.

Your correspondence. Include a copy of the email you sent to your winning bidder when the auction closed. This document has all the pertinent information about the auction.

Recycling information. If you're shipping passels of packing peanuts, let buyers know where they can recycle them. You can find a list of foam-packaging recycling locations at from the Plastic Loose Fill Council at www.loosefillpackaging.com. Or direct your buyer to the council's hotline at 800-828-2214.

A postcard. If you live in an interesting or picturesque area, include a short thank-you note on the back of a local postcard.

More information. Do you have information about a bug fix or update to a piece of software or hardware you've sold? Have some suggestions on how to care for the item or how best to clean or handle it? If you have some additional information that might prove useful to the buyer, include it. The buyer will appreciate it.

Some munchies. Consider tossing in a few mints or hard candies in a small plastic bag. Just don't include anything that might melt in the heat.

Disguise Valuables

If you're shipping electronics or camera equipment in its original box, consider doing what mail-order retailers do to discourage theft: wrap the box with kraft paper or put it inside another box.

Get the Address Right

Many shipping companies, including UPS and FedEx, will not deliver to a post office box. Be sure the buyer's address is acceptable to the shipper you're using.

Going Multiple

If your shipment consists of several pieces and you feel you can't ship them safely or economically in one box, pack the pieces separately in as many boxes as needed. Be sure to let your buyer know to expect several boxes, and mark each box to indicate that it's part of a multiple-item shipment— *1 of 2, 2 of 2*, and so on.

To Leave or Not to Leave

Some shippers will leave packages at a buyer's door even if nobody is home to sign for them. This may not be a problem for most people, but it won't hurt to ask a buyer if theft is a concern. Perhaps you can notify the shipper to drop the package at the back, not the front, door. Maybe the buyer would prefer a signature required for delivery, as described at right (this may cost extra). Work out these details with your buyer to make the transaction as smooth as possible.

Consider the Climate

If you're shipping something that could be damaged by excessive heat or cold, consider using a fast shipping method as opposed to a cheaper, slow-boat method. Or plan your auctions so that you're selling sensitive items during the spring or fall, when temperatures may be more moderate.

Sign Here: Signature Confirmation

If you'd like an additional layer of protection for your shipment, you can require that an individual at the shipping address will sign for the package. This add-on service is called *signature confirmation*.

If you're purchasing postage at a post office, signature confirmation costs an additional $1.80. If you're purchasing postage online, signature confirmation costs $1.30.

In order to be covered by the PayPal Seller Protection Policy (see page 119), all shipments valued at $250 or higher must have signature confirmation added.

Special Packing Considerations

Photos and unbreakable flat items. Use manila or bubble-lined envelopes with a same-size piece of cardboard for stiffening the package. For particularly old or delicate flat merchandise, consider putting the item in a plastic sleeve, then sandwiching it between two pieces of cardboard. Instead of licking the adhesive on the envelope to close it, use a strip of clear packing tape to seal it. If the item is large, you might send it in a mailing tube, provided it isn't too brittle to withstand being rolled up. Use a sturdy tube and secure the end caps with strapping tape.

Framed items. Disassemble framed art and pack each component separately using the techniques above. Wrap the corners of the frame with foam sheets or foam corners to prevent damage. You can buy boxes made for shipping framed items.

If you doubt your ability to properly pack large or valuable artwork (or anything else, for that matter), hire a packaging professional, such as The Packaging Store (www. packagingstore.com), which has locations nationwide.

Computers and electronics. As noted on page 121, avoid using fill that can generate a static charge—no newspaper, Styrofoam peanuts, or crumpled kraft paper.

Glassware and other breakables. Wrap the item in tissue paper, then in bubble wrap. Put it in a box large enough to accommodate lots of shock-absorbing packing peanuts. Place this box inside a larger box and add a cushion of packing peanuts around the smaller box.

Antique dolls. Fragile dolls have unique packing requirements. The gurus at Debra's Dolls (www.debrasdolls.com) take some impressive measures to protect their shipments: "Dolls that have sleep eyes (eyes that open and close) will have their wigs removed and the inside of their heads packed with tissue paper to secure the eye rockers during transit. Dolls with sleep eyes that also have solid dome heads will have their heads removed and then packed with tissue paper." You may or may not want to go to those extremes, but you should at least wrap the arms, head, and legs separately. Consider wrapping a disposable diaper around the doll's head, then wrapping the entire doll in bubble wrap.

And speaking of Pampers. We've found disposable diapers to be an increasingly useful part of our packing arsenal. They do a great job of cushioning hard-to-protect appendages—such as doll heads.

And because *someone* out there just made a wisecrack, yes, we are referring to new, unused disposable diapers.

Stinky stuff. If your item has a musty, smoky, or otherwise unpleasant odor, wrap it in layers of tissue paper before wrapping it in bubble wrap. The tissue will help absorb the odor; bubble wrap alone would simply seal the odor in.

More Shipping and Packing Tips

Tips for Labeling

Other labeling tools

You don't use Microsoft Word? With Avery's online label-formatting service (www.avery.com/print), you can create formatted labels using your Web browser. Numerous label-printing programs are available for Windows and Macs alike, and many database and address book programs can also do the job.

Get the abbreviations right

Just some of the fascinating reads on the USPS Web site are lists of two-letter state abbreviations and street suffixes. See www.usps.com/ncsc/lookups/usps_abbreviations.htm. You don't have to worry about correct abbreviations if you create labels through the USPS site; it supplies them and the recipient's nine-digit ZIP code for you.

Size it right

Don't buy labels that are smaller than approximately four by six inches. You want to have plenty of room to clearly print or write both the recipient's address as well as your complete return address. (And yes, we recommend putting the return address and recipient's address on one label rather than using a separate return address label.)

Position it properly

To help ensure that it won't come loose in transit, try to avoid placing your label over any box seams or packaging tape. Use clear packaging tape over the label to keep it dry and secure, but if you've printed pre-paid shipping labels, don't tape over any barcodes.

International issues

When labeling a package for international shipment, be sure to include the destination country and the buyer's contact phone number. (For more information on international shipping, see page 130.)

Tips for International Shipping

Surviving the paperwork

Regardless of the carrier you use, shipping internationally requires more paperwork.

For the US Postal Service, customs-declaration paperwork must accompany your shipment. Depending on the weight and value of your shipment and on how you send it, you'll complete either form 2976 or 2976-A. These forms are available at your local post office. You can also find them online at www.usps.com/global/customs.htm. (Starting in late 2005, you can also print international labels, complete customs forms, and purchase shipping using your eBay account. For updates on this welcome development, see www.ebaymatters.com.)

For UPS and FedEx, you'll need to complete a commercial invoice, which, like the USPS's forms, lists the contents and value of the shipment.

When filling out a declaration form or commercial invoice, there's no need to be overly specific about a shipment's contents. For example, *comic book* is preferable to *Uncanny X-Men #94*. What's most important is the accuracy of the declared value.

This brings up an interesting question. What if you paid $12 for an item at a thrift shop, then sold it on eBay for $90? Experienced international sellers say that it's legal and acceptable to declare what *you* paid. The exception: If your buyer wants to insure for the actual purchase price, declare the item's final auction price. (And if the auction closed at a price below the retail value, declare the lower value.)

Important: In an effort to save money on duty and import fees, a buyer may try to persuade you to fib on these forms. Don't do it. The penalties for falsifying information on customs forms are big, and these days, governments take exports and imports very seriously. Always walk the straight and narrow when it comes to doing business.

Tips for Packing Large Items

Heavy or large items have unique packing requirements, and freight companies won't take a package that doesn't meet these requirements. If you aren't willing or able to build a crate, or you don't have heavy-duty boxes, you might want to contract with a shipper that provides packing services. (You can choose this option when working your way through eBay's Freight Resource Center screens.) You'll pay more for shipping, but you'll sleep easier knowing that your shipment is properly protected.

Pack locally

Another option is to have a packing service near you do your packaging. Chances are a local packing service will charge less than a freight company, and you can often arrange for the freight company to pick up from the packing service.

Going it alone

One of the great things about the Freight Resource Center is that it automatically searches dozens of trucking companies to find the one that meets your mix of location, destination, item, and packing requirements.

If you'd rather pick your own shipper and work directly with it, here's a list of sites to get you started.

Get docked

Neither of our houses has a loading dock, and we doubt yours does, either. That means using shippers that provide liftgate service—they'll bring a truck equipped with a motorized platform that will raise and lower your shipment. Liftgate service often costs extra, so if you can transport your item to a packing service that has a loading dock, you may save yourself some dough.

Box better

If you're shipping heavy items in cardboard boxes, try to use boxes whose seams are stitched or stapled rather than glued. And use dense cushioning material, such as molded foam—a heavy load can crush foam peanuts or crumpled paper. Use strapping tape to seal heavy boxes.

If you frequently ship heavy items, you might investigate *foam-in-place* packaging systems. With foam-in-place packaging, a liquid foam is injected into a plastic bag that you place in a box. The foam then molds to fit the shape of whatever you put on top of the bag. To learn more, do a Web search for *foam in place* or visit www.instapak.com.

Site	Comments
www.freightcenter.com	Get quotes and compare rates from numerous shippers.
www.cratersandfreighters.com	Provides packing services; numerous locations nationwide.
www.roadway.com	Large trucking company's site contains great information for first-time shippers.
www.oldgloryfreight.com	Freight agency matches carriers to shipments.
www.fedex.com/us/freight/main/	Provides guaranteed on-time delivery.

When Things Go Wrong: Solving Problems

We've said it before and we'll say it again: most eBayers are honest people, and most eBay transactions take place without a hitch.

Most of them. Problems happen, and when they do, even the best-planned auction can go to pieces.

But just because you're having a problem doesn't necessarily mean that your auction is doomed. A couple of diplomatic emails can often iron out a wrinkle, and you can also pick up the phone and make a call if you care to.

If you aren't able to resolve a problem, you may find yourself agonizing over whether to leave negative feedback. It's a tricky decision—warning other sellers about a problem bidder is a good idea, but at the same time, a bidder may leave negative feedback for you in retaliation. Sometimes it's better to clench your teeth and walk away.

At right, you'll find headings that describe the most common problems you may encounter. Below each heading are some recommendations for dealing with that problem.

Even if you aren't able to resolve a problem, you may be able to salvage your auction by using eBay's Second Chance Offer option, which lets you offer your item to other bidders who didn't win the auction. If that isn't an option, you can always relist your item.

Buyer Doesn't Respond

You sent an email invoice when the auction ended, and a reminder email three days after that. And still nothing.

One last chance. Wait about a week after the auction has closed, then send a final reminder. We include the words *FINAL REMINDER* in the Subject line. Be firm but diplomatic:

This is to remind you that you are the winning bidder on my eBay auction for a Palm V (8mb) w/2 cradles (item #39484737). Your high bid is $74.66 plus $8.50 for shipping and $2.20 for insurance, total $85.36.

It's important to let me know how and when you intend to make payment. As per the auction description, payment is due within 10 days of completion. As high bidder on an auction, you have entered into a binding contract to purchase this item, as per eBay's rules. Please be in touch as soon as possible.

You might want to check your buyer's feedback for a pattern of negatives (see page 23 for instructions on looking at a member's feedback). If there is a history of negative feedback, you may be in for a hard time. Consider blocking that bidder from future auctions if things don't work out (page 100). If there isn't a pattern of recent negatives, be patient—your buyer may be in a jam and may need more time to pay up, or may even have to back out of the deal.

Now what? If you don't hear from the bidder within ten days—or if you get an email that simply says "cancel my order" (this happened to us once)—consider filing an Unpaid Item dispute, as described on page 142. Next, relist your item or make a Second Chance Offer, then apply for a final value fee credit. See the following pages for instructions.

Buyer Backs Out

Buyers will sometimes be unable to complete a transaction.

Legitimate excuse. If a buyer has a reasonable excuse for backing out and lets you know promptly, don't leave negative feedback. If the auction had other bidders, consider a Second Chance offer (see page 140). If there were no other bidders, you can relist your item and request a final value fee credit, after reaching a mutual agreement with the buyer through the Unpaid Item process (see page 143).

Lame excuse. If it appears that the buyer has wasted your time, consider leaving negative feedback, but note that you may receive negative feedback in return. Sometimes it's best to just walk away.

Now what? File an Unpaid Item dispute. Once you've completed the process, you can relist or make a Second Chance Offer.

Buyer's Check Bounces

There's usually no excuse for this. But banks do err, and so do their depositors.

It's worth emailing the buyer once more to say that the check bounced and to offer the opportunity to make immediate payment using PayPal or by sending a money order via overnight mail or FedEx.

Now what? If the buyer doesn't make good, negative feedback is in order. Initiate an Unpaid Item dispute and, once it's completed, either relist your item or make a Second Chance offer.

Buyer Initiates Chargeback

A chargeback is initiated by a credit card issuer (a bank, for instance) to reverse charges on a transaction that previously cleared. Chargebacks are designed to protect credit card users. If you order something and never receive it, if you receive something that differs from its original description, or if your credit card is stolen and then used, you can gripe to your credit card company, and it will issue a chargeback.

Unfortunately, fraudulent chargebacks are a risk you take when accepting payments through online payment services, such as PayPal. You can be victimized by a fraudulent chargeback months after you've shipped an item.

PayPal's Seller Protection Policy is designed to protect sellers from fraudulent chargebacks. If you follow PayPal's rules to the letter, you'll be covered. Those rules include shipping to the address shown on PayPal's Transaction Details page, and retaining proof of shipment. (Get all the details from PayPal's online Help—search for *seller protection*.)

Don't let a buyer tempt you into breaking these rules. For example, a buyer may ask you to ship an item to her work address because "it's a present for my husband." If that address isn't the one on the Transaction Details page, you've instantly lost seller protection.

Now what? If you feel you've been stung by an inappropriate or fraudulent chargeback, PayPal will try to help you work things out. If a buyer has initiated a chargeback, PayPal is notified by the credit card company. After you are notified, use the Resolution Center in your PayPal account to resolve the situation.

Turning to the Telephone

You may want to pick up the phone to try to work out a problem. We've only had to do this once, but it was worth the effort: we ironed out a payment problem in minutes, and a potentially sour deal turned sweet.

If you've been exchanging emails with a buyer, ask him or her to send a phone number.

If the buyer is unresponsive, get the number from eBay. Click the Advanced Search link, under the Search button on any eBay page. In the Search page, click the Find Contact Information link.

You'll need to supply your buyer's User ID as well as your auction's item number—personal information is available only to the parties involved in an auction. Enter this information in and click the Search button. You'll receive an email from eBay containing the bidder's name, city, state, and phone number.

Note: The bidder will also receive an email containing your contact information, including your phone number. Receiving this email may, in and of itself, inspire the buyer to get in touch.

If you're dealing with an unresponsive bidder, don't feel that you must make a phone call. If you're uncomfortable making a call or having someone get your contact information, don't bother.

When the Worst Happens: Making Insurance Claims

You packed your item within an inch of its life, yet it arrived at its new home damaged—or it never arrived at all.

If you followed our advice, you shipped the item with insurance or used a shipper that automatically insures packages up to a certain value. (We typically require insurance when shipping anything worth more than about $40.)

Regardless of whether the item was insured, reply to the buyer immediately to apologize and issue a refund or replacement, if you have one. Ask the buyer how he or she would like to receive the refund. Typically, we refund payments by money order or check. If you refund via PayPal and the buyer has a Premier or Business account, PayPal takes a cut and the buyer won't be fully refunded.

And then what? That's tricky. Filing and following through on a claim can be a time-consuming adventure that requires involving your buyer—as if he or she hasn't suffered enough. If the item was fairly inexpensive, it may be easier for everyone if you forgo the claim. Consider it self insurance. If the item is inexpensive and you have a duplicate, consider sending it on to the buyer. Whatever you decide, be sure you make restitution to the buyer as soon as possible. Don't make a buyer wait for your shipper to issue you a refund. Filing a claim is generally worthwhile only if substantial cash is involved.

Filing a Claim with the US Postal Service

If the item was damaged in transit, you must involve the buyer in your claim. Ask the buyer to take the item and all the packaging to his or her local post office. There, the buyer can begin filling out a damage claim form that will be forwarded on to you.

For either a loss or damage claim, go to any post office armed with the following.

Proof of insurance. The original mailing and insurance receipt are the tickets here. If you print postage online (page 127), always save the printed receipt.

Proof of value. You'll need to present evidence of the value of the item, such as a sales receipt or invoice.

For a damage claim, you will need to wait until the buyer's post office has forwarded the claim form to you.

And for a loss claim, you'll need a signed letter or statement from the buyer saying he or she never received the package. The letter must be dated at least 21 days from the mailing date.

If you purchased insurance online and there is no electronic record of delivery, this letter can also serve as proof of loss.

The fine print. When you're filing a claim for damage or partial loss of contents, you must do so within 60 days of the date of mailing. If you're filing for a complete loss, the filing period varies according to the service you used. To learn more, go to www.usps.com/insuranceclaims.

The Postal Service usually pays claims within 30 days. Claims for $50 or less are paid by the post office you submit them to. Claims of more than $50 are handled nationally and often take longer.

Keep in mind that when the Postal Service pays on a claim, it assumes ownership of your item, whether it's salvageable or not, and it's entirely likely that you'll never get it back.

Filing a Claim with UPS

The process for filing a claim with UPS is slightly less rigorous. You can file a claim via UPS's online customer service or you can call and speak to someone.

In either case, once you've reported a claim, you'll receive a Damage/Loss Notification letter with a claim number. You have up to six months after the scheduled delivery date to ask UPS to take action. Once you receive notification, whether filing a damage or loss claim, you will need to fax the completed claim form, the original UPS shipment paperwork, and documentation that confirms the value of the item.

If you're filing a damage claim, you'll need to have the buyer return the broken item and all packaging, since UPS may require an inspection to approve your refund. Be sure to reimburse the buyer's return shipping costs. Make the process as easy as possible for him or her. Typically, once UPS receives all the appropriate paperwork, your refund will be mailed within five business days.

Filing a Claim with FedEx

You can file a claim with FedEx online or by mail or fax. If you have a FedEx account and you file your claim online, FedEx throws in a swell perk—periodic email updates on the status of your claim.

Another plus: FedEx will partially complete the online claim form for you based on the shipping data already in its system.

FedEx will want a completed claim form, a copy of your original shipping documentation, proof of merchandise value, and any serial numbers you may have for the item.

You must file a damage claim within 21 days of the delivery date. For a loss claim, you must file the claim within nine months from the date you shipped the package. FedEx says it typically resolves claims within five to seven days after receiving all necessary documentation. And if you're filing a damage claim, FedEx may want to inspect the item and its packaging, so be prepared to ask the buyer to return everything.

Surveying Insurance Costs

What does shipping insurance cost? It depends on the carrier and on the value of what you're shipping. Here are some ballpark rates for the Postal Service, UPS, and FedEx.

Notice, too, how the maximum insured value amounts vary from carrier to carrier—something to think about when auctioning those diamond necklaces.

US Postal Service

Priority Mail. No insurance is included with the base postage rates. Insurance for items valued at $50 or less is $1.30; $200 or less is $3.20; and each additional $100 insured value or fraction thereof is an additional $1.00, up to $5,000 per package.

Express Mail. Express Mail packages are insured for up to $100. Additional coverage per $100 insured value or fraction thereof is $1.00, up to $5,000 per package.

UPS

Packages are automatically insured against loss or damage for up to $100. Additional insurance for packages valued between $100.01 and $300 costs $1.20, and an additional 40 cents per $100 of insured value or fraction thereof. As with FedEx, the maximum insured value is $50,000.

FedEx

Both FedEx Express and Ground services give you $100 of coverage. Additional insurance for FedEx Ground costs $1.20 for packages valued between $100.01 and $300, and an additional 40 cents per $100 of insured value or fraction thereof. Additional coverage for FedEx Express costs $2.50 for packages valued at $100 to $500, and an additional 50 cents for each additional $100 insured value or fraction thereof. The maximum declared value for FedEx Ground and FedEx Express services is $50,000.

Bouncing Back: Second Chance Offers

So it's come to this, has it? Your auction didn't work out, maybe for one of the reasons listed on the previous pages. You have our sympathies—we've been there, and it's frustrating.

But eBay life goes on, and one of your first priorities will likely be to salvage your auction. When a buyer backs out of a deal or just vanishes, eBay gives you another chance—the Second Chance Offer.

You can offer to sell your item to any one of the other bidders who participated in the item's original auction. (So yes, one of *them* gets a second chance, too.) You can make a Second Chance Offer within 60 days after the auction closed. It goes without saying (but we'll say it anyway) that you must have at least one under-bidder in order to make a Second Chance Offer. If your auction ended with one Buy It Now bid and that buyer backed out, you can't make a Second Chance Offer.

But don't take this path until you're certain that your original buyer isn't going to come through. You're in for some uncomfortable explaining if you promise your item to another bidder and then receive payment and an apologetic letter from the original bidder the next day.

Here's how to make lemonade from auction lemons.

Making a Second Chance Offer

To make a Second Chance Offer, go to your original auction listing and click the Second Chance Offer link—you'll find it near the top of the page.

Other actions for this item:

You can manage all your items in <u>My eBay</u> and do the following:

- 📦 <u>Mark the item shipped</u>.
- ☆ <u>Leave feedback</u> for this item.
- ✉ <u>Contact the buyer</u>, liberomalins, about this item.

Additional Options:

- ▪ Send a non-winning bidder a <u>second chance offer</u> if you have more than one of this item.
- ▪ To list another item like this one, use the <u>Sell Similar</u> option.
- ▪ To list this specific item again, use the <u>Relist</u> option.
- ▪ Customize your seller settings by updating <u>seller preferences</u>.

The Second Chance Offer page appears, complete with a reminder that you should try to work out a problem with the original high bidder.

My Messages: Second Chance Offer

Second Chance Offer lets you offer an item to the bidder or bidders who didn't win it. <u>Learn More</u>

- Sending a Second Chance Offer is free but if your item sells, you will be charged a Final Value Fee based on a percentage of the final sale price.
- You can send a Second Chance Offer for up to 60 days after the listing ends.
- Before making a Second Chance Offer, try and work things out with your winning bidder first.

Please enter the item number below and click on the **Continue** button.

Item number

5782502224

Continue >

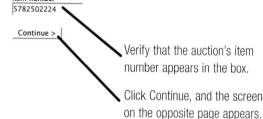

Verify that the auction's item number appears in the box.

Click Continue, and the screen on the opposite page appears.

Choose a time limit on your offer: 1 day, 3 days, 5 days, or 7 days.

If your auction had several bidders, each bidder appears here. Choose the one who gets the offer. If the checkbox next to a particular User ID is disabled, that bidder has chosen to not receive Second Chance Offer notifications.

The Second Chance Offer price is based on the maximum bid a bidder made during the auction.

After you've chosen a bidder and duration, click Continue. Review the summary screen that appears next, and if all is in order, click its Send button. To make changes, click the Back button.

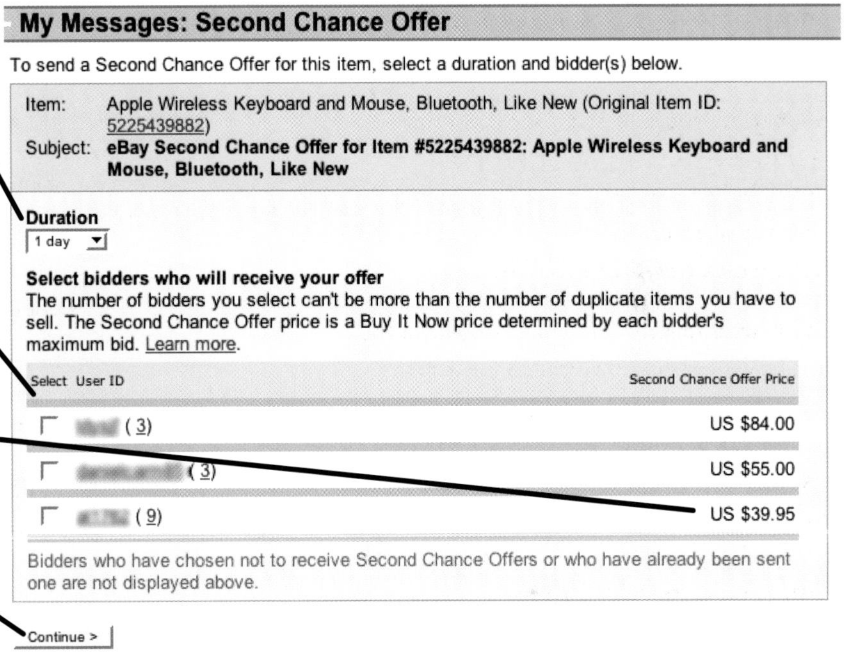

My Messages: Second Chance Offer

To send a Second Chance Offer for this item, select a duration and bidder(s) below.

Item:	Apple Wireless Keyboard and Mouse, Bluetooth, Like New (Original Item ID: 5225439882)
Subject:	**eBay Second Chance Offer for Item #5225439882: Apple Wireless Keyboard and Mouse, Bluetooth, Like New**

Duration

[1 day ▼]

Select bidders who will receive your offer

The number of bidders you select can't be more than the number of duplicate items you have to sell. The Second Chance Offer price is a Buy It Now price determined by each bidder's maximum bid. Learn more.

Select	User ID	Second Chance Offer Price
☐	■■■■ (3)	US $84.00
☐	■■■■■■■ (3)	US $55.00
☐	■■■■ (9)	US $39.95

Bidders who have chosen not to receive Second Chance Offers or who have already been sent one are not displayed above.

Continue >

Second Chance Details

What does it cost? eBay doesn't charge additional listing fees for a Second Chance Offer. If a bidder accepts your offer, you will have to pay a final value fee based on the final purchase price.

No deal? If you make a Second Chance Offer and the offer expires without a sale, you can make another offer to a different bidder.

Have another? You can use Second Chance Offers if you have more than one of a given item. For example, if you have two identical Incredible Hulk lunchboxes, you can use a Second Chance Offer to sell the second one to an under-bidder.

Other paths to a second chance. You can also send a Second Chance Offer by clicking the Bid History link on your completed auction page. And finally, you can also get to the Second Chance Offer by clicking the Second Chance Offer link in the Action drop-down menu for the listing in My eBay.

Disaster Recovery: Report and Refund

If a buyer weasels out of a deal or sends you a rubber check, you can open an Unpaid Item dispute. When you begin the Unpaid Item process, eBay opens official lines of communication between you and the (deadbeat) buyer.

We don't take this step for every sour auction, and neither should you. Once you start to escalate, even when you're in the right, you risk receiving negative feedback.

One factor that may force your hand is that you must go through the Unpaid Item process in order to request a Final Value Fee (FVF) credit. If you auctioned a big-ticket item, you probably want that fee back.

Opening an Unpaid Item Dispute

You can begin the process between eight and 45 days after an auction has ended. Begin by jotting down the item number of your problem auction (or select it and choose your browser's Copy command).

Next, head to the eBay site map. In the Dispute Console area, click the Report an Unpaid Item Dispute link. You'll probably be asked to sign in, and once you do, the Dispute Console screen appears. Click the Report an Unpaid Item link.

Read the page's fine print, and then type or paste the item number into the Item Number box and click Continue.

A new page appears containing a couple of pop-up menus that let you describe why you're filing the dispute. Unless you and the buyer have already been in touch about nullifying the auction, you'll want to choose the option called *The buyer has not paid for the item*.

After you choose the appropriate options and click the Continue button, both you and your delinquent bidder will receive an email. What happens next depends on the type of dispute you filed—and on how the bidder responds.

Friendly Reminder

If you told eBay that you are filing a dispute because the buyer has not paid, the buyer will receive what eBay calls "a friendly reminder." The buyer has three response options.

I want to pay now. The buyer pays for the item using one of the methods you accept. If the buyer pays via PayPal, the dispute is closed automatically. If the buyer pays by another method, wait until you receive payment (and it clears) before you close the dispute through the Dispute Console link under My eBay views in My eBay.

I already paid. The buyer must provide payment information for you to review. If payment has been made to your satisfaction, choose the appropriate option to close the dispute.

Communicate with seller. Choosing this option opens lines of communication, through an eBay web page, between you and the buyer. Do your best to work things out, but you aren't obligated to participate in a pointless conversation. Once a buyer has responded at least once, you can choose to close the dispute.

Mutual Agreement

If you stated that you and the buyer have come to a mutual agreement to nullify the auction, the buyer receives a notification asking him or her to respond in one of two ways.

Agree. If the buyer confirms that he or she has come to a mutual agreement with you, you'll receive your FVF credit, the buyer will not receive an Unpaid Item strike, and the auction will be put out of its misery. Aside from getting paid, this is the best outcome you can hope for.

Disagree. If the buyer disagrees that you've reached a mutual agreement, you will not receive a FVF credit and the buyer will not receive an Unpaid Item strike. eBay closes the dispute and you can't file another Unpaid Item claim for that item. At this point, you must either continue to pursue the buyer or chalk up your FVF as

a loss (and make a Second Chance offer or relist your item).

If the buyer doesn't respond after seven days, you can close the dispute and receive your FVF credit. The buyer, however, does not receive a strike. (And frankly, we're unclear as to why the buyer isn't punished for ignoring you. But we don't make the rules, we just report them.)

However, if you feel your buyer is an honest sort and you can put this auction out of its misery, this is the route to take to get your credit.

Case Closed

If the buyer has responded once or hasn't responded at all after one week, you can choose to close the dispute through the Dispute Console.

When you go to the Dispute Console page, you'll see all disputes that are still open. Those disputes that are eligible for closure have a checkmark next to them. We've found that it can take up to ten days of buyer silence before eBay allows you to wrap things up.

When you choose to close a dispute, eBay requires you to select a reason for doing so.

We've agreed not to complete the transaction. You and the buyer both want to walk away from the auction. The buyer doesn't receive an Unpaid Item strike and you receive your FVF credit.

We've completed the transaction and we're both satisfied. All's right with the world. No need for credits or strikes.

I no longer wish to communicate with or wait for the seller. You've had enough of this foolishness. The buyer gets an Unpaid Item strike, you get your FVF credit, and you're eligible to relist the item.

Note: You have 60 days after the completion of your auction to keep a dispute open. After that time, eBay closes it for you. Don't let disputes languish—you won't get your FVF credit and the buyer walks away unscathed.

Feeling Defrauded?

If you feel you've been defrauded or scammed by a bidder, you have avenues to explore. eBay provides some suggestions and links at http://pages.ebay.com/help/tp/isgw-fraud-defrauded-sellers.html.

CHAPTER 7

The Next Step

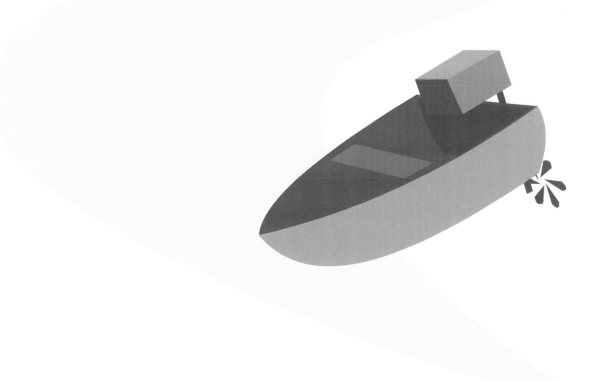

Efficiency Experts: eBay's Seller Tools

If you create a couple of auctions per week, chances are that My eBay provides all the auction-management features you need. But when your selling hobby becomes more of a habit—or even a career—it's time to consider some advanced seller tools.

There are plenty to choose from. Some tools are standalone programs that run on your PC or Mac. Others are Web-based systems that you access using your browser. Some tools are free; others have monthly subscription fees.

Regardless of how they're packaged and priced, all seller tools are aimed at making you more efficient and organized. Some tools automate the process of creating multiple listings—no need to repeatedly slog through the Sell Your Item pages that we described in Chapter 2. You'll also find tools that help you track inventory, manage pictures, print shipping labels, automate sending email and leaving feedback, and more.

Here, we spotlight eBay's own Turbo Lister, Selling Manager, Selling Manager Pro, and Blackthorne. Use these profiles as starting points for your own research. Test-drive the tools that sound appealing (free trials are usually available); that's the best way to find the tool that provides the right mix of features for your budget and selling needs.

eBay's Offerings

Turbo Lister (Windows only). This free program lets you create listings offline and then upload them to eBay in bulk. And we mean bulk—you can create and upload up to 3,000 listings.

Turbo Lister uses a series of screens to walk you through the creation of each listing. Creating listings with Turbo Lister is faster and more efficient than using your Web browser.

With Turbo Lister's built-in HTML editor, it's easy to format text, create bulleted lists, and so on. You can even preview a listing directly within Turbo Lister—no need to connect to the Internet first.

Turbo Lister is also packed with time-saving options. If you're selling a bunch of similar items, you can duplicate one listing and then change the required specifics. You can also specify your preferred settings for auction duration, starting price, listing upgrades, payment instructions, and more. Once you've set up these defaults, you don't have to manually enter them for each auction. You can even have Turbo Lister automatically enter a passage of text (such as your payment policies) in every listing you create.

To find out more and download Turbo Lister, click the Site Map link at the top of any eBay page, then, in the Selling Tools area, click the Turbo Lister link.

Selling Manager (Windows/Mac). Take My eBay's All Selling page and send it to business school, and you have Selling Manager. Selling Manager isn't a separate program that you download; instead, it's a subscription-based service that actually replaces the All Selling page in My eBay.

Summary

Last updated on Aug-21-05 11:32:44 PDT.

Quick Stats	GMS	# of listings
Scheduled Listings		**0**
▪ Starting within the next hour		0
▪ Starting today		0
Active Listings	$0.00	**0**
▪ Closing within the next hour		0
▪ Closing today		0
▪ Items with Questions		0
Ended Listings		**9**
Sold Items	$147.43	**8**
▪ Awaiting Payment		2
▪ Paid and ready to ship		3
▪ Paid and waiting for feedback		2
▪ Paid and shipped		3

With Selling Manager, you can customize email templates, print shipping labels and invoices, and track sales, among other activities. Combine it with Turbo Lister, and you can create and keep track of auctions quickly and efficiently.

At this writing, eBay charges a $4.99 monthly subscription fee to use Selling Manager. The first 30 days are free, so you can take it for a test drive. However, if you decide not to use it, you'll need to unsubscribe; otherwise eBay will automatically begin charging your account after the 30 days are up.

To check out Selling Manager, go to the eBay site map and, in the Selling Tools area, click the Selling Manager link.

Selling Manager Pro (Windows/Mac). If you find yourself knocking on the PowerSeller door (see page 153), consider Selling Manager Pro. At $15.99 per month, it's pricier than Selling Manager, but it does much more. Selling Manager Pro streamlines workflow for high-volume sellers by adding inventory management, reporting, statistics, and even automated feedback features. A 30-day trial is available.

Both versions of Selling Manager run on any computer with an Internet connection and Internet Explorer 4 or later, Netscape 4 or later, or America Online 3 or later. We've also found they work quite nicely in Firefox and Apple's Safari.

Blackthorne (Windows only). Blackthorne is an update to Seller's Assistant, one of eBay's original seller tools. Blackthorne Basic ($9.99 per month) allows you to use templates to create auctions offline and batch-upload them. It also includes other tools, including sales tracking, customizable email templates, and a bulk relisting feature. Blackthorne Pro ($24.99 per month) adds support for multiple users, inventory management tools, sorting and filtering features, invoicing and shipping tools, and more.

eBay offers a free 30-day trial period for both programs; see www.ebay.com/blackthorne. **Note:** At this writing, the Blackthorne programs are in a prerelease, *beta-test* form. If you prefer to use Seller's Assistant, you can still sign up for the service at www.ebay.com/sellers_assistant. But note that eBay has announced that it will eventually "retire" the Seller's Assistant tools.

Comparing eBay's Offerings

How do these offerings stack up? For a comparison of the features each provides, see www.ebay.com/selling_manager/comparison.html.

And note that you can move from one tool to another as your needs change. For example, Blackthorne can import saved items from Turbo Lister, and Selling Manager Pro can import items from Seller's Assistant Pro. Similarly, Blackthorne Basic and Pro can import from Turbo Lister.

Accounting Assistant (Windows only). Want to import your eBay and PayPal transaction information directly into Intuit's QuickBooks accounting software? Consider Accounting Assistant. It's free, provided you subscribe to one of the Seller's Assistant, Selling Manager, or Blackthorne tools. (And, of course, you'll need a copy of QuickBooks.)

To learn more, see www.ebay.com/accountingassistant.

Other eBay Tools From Around the Web

An entire industry has sprung up around eBay, and seller tools form a big part of it. Image hosting, auction management, advanced reporting, bulk listing programs—there are dozens of programs and services aimed at improving your bottom line.

Most of them also require that you give up part of that bottom line, but as with eBay's offerings, trial versions of most of these programs and services are available.

Here's a sampling of our favorites. To keep up with the always-changing eBay tools scene, check out www.auctionsoftwarereview.com. You'll also find a useful directory of eBay tools at AuctionBytes (www.auctionbytes.com). And don't forget to stop in on our site (www.ebaymatters.com) for links, updates, and tidbits on eBay.

Andale (Windows/Mac). Andale, the company that provides those free page counters (page 105), offers a wide variety of products. Andale Lister is a Web-based tool that handles auction listing, inventory management, and scheduling. Andale Checkout helps to automate payment, customer contact, and shipping processes. Monthly fees for each of these services start at $2.

Andale Images is an image-hosting service that helps you organize and upload auction photos. Rates for image hosting begin at $3 per month for 3MB of storage. Andale also offers a variety of mix-and-match payment options that let you choose the plans and services you need. **www.andale.com**.

Auction Hawk (Windows/Mac). Auction Hawk provides image hosting and Web-based auction-management tools. The Basic plan starts at $12.99 per month and allows for 25MB of storage and approximately 110 listings. Pricier plans provide more features, such as inventory management, profit/loss reports, and additional storage space. There is also an image hosting-only option. A free, 21-day trial is available. **www.auctionhawk.com**.

MarketBlast (Windows/Mac). This $99 program provides 100 ad templates along with an HTML editor to modify or create templates. MarketBlast lets you keep track of inventory, organize listings into folders, update listings, and more. MarketBlast works with Flickr (www.flickr.com), the online photo management and sharing site, enabling you to use Flickr to store and host auction photos. Flickr offers unlimited storage with upload limits of 20MB per month (free) or 2GB per month ($24.95 yearly).

A free but feature-limited demo version of MarketBlast is available. **www.marketblast.com**.

iSale (Mac only). If you're running Mac OS X 10.3 or a later version, this $39.95 program offers some interesting options. iSale taps into Apple's iPhoto digital photography program and iCal scheduling software. If you have an Apple .Mac account, you can upload auction photos to your iDisk: no need to pay eBay for image storage. You can prepare auctions offline, track active auctions, generate multiple auctions at once, and more. **www.equinux.com**.

Vendio (Windows/Mac). Vendio provides a full line of Web-based listing-creation, auction-management, and image-hosting tools. Vendio Image Hosting packages start at $2.95 per month for 3MB of image storage. Vendio Sales Manager is a Web-based listing and sales automation tool that includes features such as free scheduled listings, US Postal Service and UPS integration, custom templates, and post-sale management.

Vendio Sales Manager comes in two flavors: Inventory Edition and Merchandising Edition. The Inventory Edition makes it possible to create or edit listings for large quantities of items, as well as schedule auctions for hundreds of items at once. The Merchandising Edition is geared toward sellers who often list single-quantity items and want more advanced merchandising features, such as automated invoicing, payment notification, and order tracking. Two-week trial versions are available. **www.vendio.com**.

Climbing the eBay Ladder

If online auctions become more than just casual endeavors for you, you might want to explore some of the advanced selling options eBay provides. You could start by creating an About Me page. It's free, and it's a great way to promote yourself and your auctions.

And if you find yourself thinking, "You know, I could sell things for other people," you might consider becoming an eBay Trading Assistant, offering your selling services to people who can't or don't want to learn everything you've just learned.

Create an About Me Page

Want to tell prospective buyers and fellow sellers a bit about yourself? Looking for a place to spell out your shipping and payment policies? eBay has set aside a slice of virtual real estate just for you: the About Me page.

The About Me page is your own home page within the eBay site. Your About Me page can contain information about you, a photo, your most recent feedback, your current listings, favorite links, eBay finds, or any combination thereof. (Just don't use this forum to promote business you do outside of eBay or items prohibited on eBay.) eBay provides three design templates to choose from, or you can customize the page with your own HTML.

Once you create an About Me page, your User ID will be accompanied by the About Me badge **me**. You'll also have your own Web address—for example, http://members.eBay.com/aboutme/mustardmaven. You can promote yourself by including this address in email messages, eBay forum postings, and elsewhere.

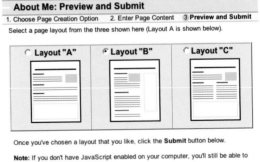

To create an About Me page, go to the eBay site map and, in the Connect area, click the About Me link. A series of screens appears that assist you in creating your page, either with eBay's help or by pasting in your own HTML coding.

Seller for Sale: Becoming a Trading Assistant

Not everyone has the patience, know-how, and inclination to become an eBay seller. But you do, and you can turn your experience into cash by helping people sell their dusty doodads on eBay.

It's called the Trading Assistant Program, and if you meet the criteria we describe shortly, you can join and be listed in the Trading Assistant Directory. If you want to trade and earn on eBay but don't have products or care to search for them, this is one alternative.

eBay doesn't collect a fee for participation in the program and you do not become an eBay employee or contractor. eBay is simply providing an avenue for its accomplished sellers to advertise their services and expertise.

But working with people to sell their goods is no small matter. Typically, a Trading Assistant charges a fee, agreed upon with the owner of the merchandise long before the first item goes up for sale. You might charge a percentage of each sale: perhaps ten percent on items under $50 and seven percent on items over $50. You'll also need to address the nuts and bolts decisions: Will you charge for transporting the items from the owner's home or place of business to yours? What will be the starting price of each auction? What if an item doesn't sell or meet its reserve price? Who will ship the items? Iron out these details before you start.

Many Trading Assistants prefer to have the goods in their possession so they can take care of all shipping chores. Keep in mind that the fees, feedback, and responsibility for these sales are all yours.

For more information about the Trading Assistant program, see the Trading Assistant Hub at www.ebay.com/tahub.

Trading Assistant criteria. To become a Trading Assistant, you must have sold at least four items in the past 30 days, have a feedback rating of 50 or higher, and at least a 97-percent positive feedback profile.

If you make the grade and are interested in signing up, go to www.ebay.com/tahub. Follow the links to apply to become a Trading Assistant, fill out the form, and click Continue.

If you're accepted, your name will appear in the Trading Assistant directory. Users will be able to search for you by going to the Trading Assistants Program home page.

At this page, users can search for assistants by ZIP code, area code, or country. Trading Assistants are listed according to their distance from the address specified on the search page, starting with the closest. To sort the results by other criteria, such as feedback rating, searchers can click the appropriate column heading.

Reaching the Top

We've reached the end of our story, and we've come a long way together—from strategizing about pricing to refining photos to appreciating the finer points of packing peanuts.

And yet there's more.

At the top of the eBay ladder, you'll find PowerSellers—eBay sellers who, by virtue of volume and great customer service, have risen to the top tier of online auctioneers. It takes a lot of effort and a lot of auctions to become a PowerSeller, but there are rewards for being one.

Even if you don't have dreams of becoming a PowerSeller, you might consider opening an eBay Store, your own virtual nook within eBay's site, where you can promote your auctions and build your business.

But as we said in the Introduction, millions of eBay sellers are quite content to simply run an auction now and then. Whether you're in this group or you plan to climb to the top of the eBay ladder, thanks for taking this trip with us. We're looking forward to leaving positive feedback for you.

A Store of Your Own: eBay Stores

You've always dreamed of opening an antique shop, baseball card store, hardware store, boutique—you name it. With eBay Stores, you can, and you don't need any bricks or mortar to do it.

An eBay Store gives you a more stable, permanent place on eBay. Instead of just having an array of listings scattered throughout eBay's vast site, you have a centralized place where people can come to browse and buy.

Buyers can shop in your store for fixed-price merchandise as well as auction-style listings—and some listings can run indefinitely. You also get a break on many of your insertion fees, the eBay Stores icon appears in all your listings, and you can cross-promote your auctions within your store. And you get your own store address, such as http://stores.ebay.com/poodlestuff.

To qualify to open a store, you must have at least 20 unique feedback ratings or be ID Verified, or have a PayPal account that's in good standing.

Opening a store isn't free (the basic subscription fee is $15.95 per month at this writing) and certainly not for the casual seller. Still interested? Browse some existing stores by going to http://stores.ebay.com. Then go to http://pages.ebay.com/storefronts/seller-landing.html. Here you can read eBay's sales pitch for stores and get the information you need to make your decision. When you're ready to hang your e-shingle, click the Open a Store Now! button.

Becoming a PowerSeller

If your sales start soaring, you may qualify as a PowerSeller. Aside from getting additional perks from eBay, buyers look at you with a different eye. Your status as a PowerSeller means you've done a lot of business on eBay and maintained an excellent feedback record. You're a good bet when it comes to safe trade.

At the same time, though, some Power-Sellers opt out of having the PowerSeller logo ⭐ **Power Seller** in their listings because they just want to be viewed as regular Joes, not as eBay wheeler-dealers. That choice is yours.

There are five PowerSeller categories, based upon average monthly sales and other criteria. To gain admission to the PowerSeller elite, you must:

- have a minimum of 100 unique feed-backs, 98 percent of them positive
- have a minimum of four listings per month, on average, for the past three months
- be an active eBay seller for 90 days or more
- have an eBay account in good standing
- do business according to eBay community values
- comply with eBay's listing policies
- have not violated three or more of any of eBay's policies in a 60-day period
- have not violated any more serious eBay policies, such as soliciting an off-site sale, in a 60-day period.

Each month, eBay calculates eligibility and notifies members via email of their PowerSeller status. As the table below shows, the higher your tier, the more attention you get from eBay.

PowerSellers get additional perks, including their own discussion boards and monthly newsletter and VIP admission to certain eBay events.

To learn more, go to eBay's site map and click the PowerSeller link, under Selling Resources.

Tier	Monthly Sales	Priority eSupport	Free Phone Support	Dedicated Account Manager
Bronze	$1,000	yes	no	no
Silver	$3,000	yes	yes (24/7)	no
Gold	$10,000	yes	yes (24/7)	yes
Platinum	$25,000	yes	yes (24/7)	yes
Titanium	$150,000	yes	yes (24/7)	yes

Appendices

Appendix A:
A Field Guide to eBay Symbols

eBay's site contains more icons and symbols than a road-map. Because there's no legend on eBay's site that describes each one, we assembled this guide to eBay's icons, symbols, badges, and buttons.

me **About Me.** Appears next to a User ID to indicate that the user has created an About Me page (page 150). To look at the page, click the icon.

Buy It Now **Buy It Now.** If you've opted to include a Buy It Now price in your auction (page 21), this symbol appears next to your auction title in search-results pages.

Changed User ID. Appears next to a User ID to let you know that the user has changed his or her ID in the past 30 days. Even when a User ID is changed, the feedback profile remains attached to the account. You can only change your User ID once per 30-day period. See page 11.

eBay Giving Works. This symbol lets buyers know that you have chosen to give a portion of the proceeds of your auction to charity (page 41).

eBay Stores. This tag next to a User ID tells you that this user has an eBay Store, which you can visit by clicking the icon.

Feedback Profiles. Every eBayer has a feedback profile. Stars of assorted colors and types are assigned to reward higher quantities of positive feedback responses (161). The number alone does not tell the whole story. Each positive feedback response is worth +1, each negative −1. Always look at a user's feedback profile to learn the specifics.

Color	Feedback Rating
☆	10 to 49
★	50 to 99
☆	100 to 499
★	500 to 999
★	1,000 to 4,999
☆	5,000 to 9,999
☆	10,000 to 24,999
☆	25,000 to 49,999
★	50,000 to 99,999
★	100,000 or higher

ID Verify. This icon, found on the ID card portion of a member's feedback profile, indicates that the user has gone through the process of having his or her identity confirmed with eBay and a third-party security company. ID Verification enables new eBayers with little feedback to conduct certain kinds of selling (page 13).

 Gift Services. If you've decided to make gift services available in your listing, this icon joins your item title on the search-results page (page 47). eBay shoppers can also choose to search for auctions that have gift services as an option.

 New Item. If an item has been listed in the past 24 hours, it's labeled by this icon on the search-results page.

NEW! **New Services.** When eBay introduces new features or services, it uses this icon to draw your attention to them.

 New User. There's a new kid on the block and he or she has been registered on eBay for 30 days or less. After 30 days, this icon disappears.

 PayPal. If you've decided to accept PayPal as one of your methods of payment (page 50), buyers see this symbol next to your item title in search-results pages. Buyers will often browse auctions that provide PayPal payment options.

 Picture. This icon, which appears to the left of an item title on the search-results page, indicates that the listing contains a picture. Many shoppers won't even look at a listing that doesn't contain at least one image.

 PowerSeller. If you see this icon next to a User ID, you're dealing with the cream of the eBay crop. To become a PowerSeller, a seller must maintain a minimum level of monthly sales and exhibit stellar business habits (page 153).

 SquareTrade. This badge indicates that a seller has registered with SquareTrade, the online dispute resolution service. This lets you know that you're doing business with a member who is committed to using mediation to resolve auction-related problems. Doing business with this seller also affords you some additional fraud protection.

Appendix B: Common Auction Abbreviations

The auction world has enough abbreviations to make a vat of alphabet soup. Here are some you might use in your auction titles or descriptions. Just try not to use too many.

This...	Stands For This...	Comments
B&W	Black and White	Can refer to a photograph, print, movie print, and so on.
BIN	Buy It Now	Lets viewers know that you have added this option.
BBC	Bottom of Back Cover	Used to direct attention to this location.
BC	Back Cover	Used to direct attention to this location.
CIB	Cartridge in Box	Lets bidders know that the item you're selling, such as a printer, has a cartridge included.
COA	Certificate of Authenticity	An approved authentication service has examined the item and provided this document.
DOA	Dead on Arrival	Will you guarantee that your item will not arrive in this condition?
Gently Used	N/A	An item that has been used but shows little or no visible signs of wear.
HTF	Hard to Find	Just be sure there aren't 20 just like it already listed.
IMO or IMHO	In My Opinion or In My Humble Opinion	Share your humble thoughts with your buyers.
LTD	Limited Edition	A relatively small number have been made in order to create value. Limited editions are typically numbered and are sometimes signed.
MIB	Mint in Box	Perfect-condition item in its original box.
MIMB	Mint in Mint Box	Perfect-condition item in its original box, which looks untouched.
MOC	Mint on Card	Perfect-condition item, such as a Hot Wheels car, that comes packaged on a card for sale.

This...	Stands For This...	Comments
MNB	Mint No Box	Perfect-condition item without its original packaging.
MWBMT	Mint with Both Mint Tags	This refers to stuffed animals that have both a hang tag and tush tag (we kid you not). The condition of both can greatly affect value.
NBW	Never Been Worn	Refers to any article of clothing or accessory that has never been used.
NC	No Cover	The item (for example, a book) is missing its cover.
NIB	New in Box	A new item in its original packaging.
NR	No Reserve	Tells potential bidders that there is no minimum price on the item.
NRFB	Never Removed from Box	An unused item.
NWT	New with Tags	Typically refers to an item of clothing or an accessory that is new with hang tags intact.
OOAK	One of a Kind	It had better be if you include this in your listing.
OOP	Out of Print	A publication that is no longer printed by any publisher.
RARE	N/A	Probably the most overused adjective on eBay—use it only if you really know it's true.
SIG	Signature	Lets potential buyers know that your item is signed
SS	Still Sealed	Item is not only in its originally packaging, it remains sealed.
TIA	Thanks in Advance	Politeness never hurts!
VHTF	Very Hard to Find	Say so only if you know it to be true.

Appendix C:
Grading Systems and Abbreviations

There is no universally accepted grading system and language. Grading systems can vary widely for different types of items and collectibles. For example, most coin dealers and collectors refer to the American Numismatic Association's grading criteria, which includes grades such as About Uncirculated (AU) and About Good (AG). You won't find these elsewhere. If you are going to assign a grade to your item, you should have done enough research to feel confident in your assessment and use of the abbreviations and grades appropriate to your item; another option is to go to an expert and have him or her grade the item for you.

Even if common terms are used to grade antique fishing lures and books, take the time to find out what each grade means within the context of the particular item.

Sometimes you may see expression like VG+, where the plus (+) or minus (-) indicates a grading between two levels. Don't let grading terms speak for your item. Everything is subjective and you should describe your item in complete detail so that there are no misunderstandings. The table below lists some of the more common grading terms.

Common Grading Terms

M, MIB	Mint, Mint in Box	This term typically refers to an item that is considered perfect, in original, flawless condition, as is its packaging.
VF	Very Fine	Similar to mint; often used to describe printed matter.
NM	Near Mint	Essentially an "as new" item. It may have been out of the box, but the use is not visible. May have a very minor flaw.
EX	Excellent	An item in excellent condition that likely has been used but is showing only expected, subtle signs of wear. There is no damage to the item.
F	Fine	Similar to excellent; often used to describe printed matter.
VG	Very Good	An item still in very good condition with a subtle flaw or two, such as a small chip or torn page corner.
G or GD	Good	This item has been used and enjoyed. It is seeing expected wear, but no major damage.
F or FR	Fair	This item has been heavily used and is showing substantial signs of wear.
P or PR	Poor	Read "falling apart before your very eyes." This item is in bad shape and is likely beyond help. May be good for parts.

Look it Up: Grading References

Want to learn about the grading standards used by specific types of collectors? Here are some resources.

General collectibles. SmartCollector provides access to online price guides and historical eBay sales data for items included in eBay's Collectibles category, including antiques, model railroading, and comics. Registration is free; see www. smartcollector.com

Antique Furniture. Considered a classic guide to evaluating furniture, *The New Fine Points of Furniture: Early American, Good, Better, Best, Superior, Masterpiece*, by Albert Sack and Deanne Levison, will teach you the finer points of fine furniture. This volume can be hard to come by, but eBay is a great place to search for it.

Books. The Independent Online Booksellers Association uses a standard of grading based on a system defined by AB Bookman years ago. See http://www. ioba.org/terms.html

Coin Collecting. Money talks, and this list—provided by the Professional Coin Grading service—will help you understand the language. www.pcgs.com/lingo.chtml

Comics. Gadzooks! If comics are your thing, get a copy of *The Official Overstreet Comic Book Grading Guide*, by Robert Overstreet. It's the standard for comic book grading and is available through many online resellers.

Fishing Lures. Get hooked. Learn the terms associated with these increasingly popular collectibles here: www.antiquelurecollectibles.com/Articles/ Factors_in_grading_lures.htm

Records. VinylWeb, the rare music collector's marketplace, has a host of resources, including a recommended book list, to help music collectors price their vinyl. See www.vinylweb.com

Sports Memorabilia and Collectibles. To find out more about the lingo of this collectible market, go to the Professional Sports Authenticator site, www.psacard. com/lingo.chtml. Have a ball.

Stamps. Learn the criteria behind stamp grading from Professional Stamp Experts, a board of philatelic consultants, at http://www.psestamp.com/Intro.chtml

Appendix D:
A New Way to Sell

Web sites are always changing, and eBay is no exception. While we were revising this book, we could hear eBay's carpenters hammering and sawing as they worked on a major remodel. The focus of their efforts: the Sell Your Item process that we described in Chapter 2. eBay's goal is to simplify the process of setting up an auction.

The new Sell Your Item process reduces the number of screens that you need to work with. Instead of clicking through five separate screens as Chapter 2 describes, you work with just a few screens. You can customize those screens to show the listing options you use most often and hide those you never use. The screens themselves are more informative, providing detailed online help and even little niceties, such as pricing information for completed auctions similar to the one you're creating. And you can save completed listings as *templates* for future reuse.

eBay takes its time when revamping major parts of its site, in part to give us eBayers a chance to adjust to the changes and comment on them. As of late 2005, the new Sell Your Item process was still in a pre-release, or *beta*, form. Its design was still in flux, and not all features were working.

Still, it's worth checking out. Although the Sell Your Item screens shown in Chapter 2 will be available for quite some time (even after the new screens are finished), eBay will eventually switch entirely to the new process.

To learn more and try out the new Sell Your Item process, go to www.ebay.com/syialpha. And for the latest updates to this new way of selling, keep tabs on our site at www.ebaymatters.com.

1.

Tell buyers about what you're selling.
- To get help: Click the name of the field or option you have a question about.
- To customize: Click a ⊕ button.

Comments   Customize   Help

Send eBay an email containing your feedback on the new screens.

Add options to, or remove them from, the Sell Your Item page. You can also customize the page by clicking the plus sign (⊕) that appears at the top of each section of the page.

The new Sell Your Item screen displays detailed online help (not shown here) that changes as you click on different areas of the page. The help column appears along the right side of your browser window. To hide or show the help column, click this button.

2.

Reconsidering the category you've chosen? Click here.

Category
- Cameras & Photo > Digital Cameras > Point & Shoot > 3.0 to 3.9 Megapixels > Change category

Pre-filled item information
Find your product: camera

This will be the title of your listing. Fill it with words about your item that buyers would enter in a search. 55 characters maximum.

When you point to text-entry boxes, some additional help appears.

If pre-filled item information is available for your item, you can click this link to display a pop-up window containing your options.

3.

Selling format ② ⊕ Add options

ⓘ Items like yours - starting price: **$1.77**, sold price: **$3.30**. Search prices of completed items...

eBay displays pricing information for completed auctions similar to yours and makes it easy to do the research we recommend on page 19.

4.

Do your shipping homework here.

Shipping ② ⊕ Add options

Cost 🗐 Research rates and services
[Flat: same cost to all buyers ▼] [Apply]
Domestic shipping services
[▼] $
[▼] $
[▼] $

Add and remove shipping services here.

When you've completed this first page, click Continue to proceed. If eBay feels you haven't maximized your listing opportunities, a Recommendations window appears with links that let you make the suggested changes. You can choose to ignore eBay's recommendations and proceed to the next, and final, page.

Sell: Review and Enhance Your Listing

Make your listing compelling
Review how your listing will appear to buyers and add features to help you sell successfully.

Comments   Edit Listing   Help

Make your listing stand out ②

Gallery picture ($0.00)
☑ Add a small version of your first picture to Search and Listings

Subtitle ($0.50)
☐ Add a subtitle (searchable by item description) to give buyers more information.

Gift Icon ($0.25)
☐ Highlight your item with a Listing Icon. These small graphical images appear next to your item's title on listings pages.

Bold ($1.00)
☐ Attract buyers' attention and set your listing apart

Border ($3.00)
☐ Outline your listing with an eye catching frame

Highlight ($5.00)
☐ Make your listing stand out with a colored band in Search results

	Item Title	PayPal	Price	Shipping	Bids	Time Listed ▾
	9 1/2" decorative plate / for display	ⓟ	$2.99	Calculate	-	Oct-08 15:54
	Handmade Ceramic Bowl Candy Dish, Ladybugs, Orange Pink	ⓟ	$9.99	$4.50	-	Oct-08 15:56
	Fornasetti milano italin ladies face gold plate / nice!	ⓟ	$25.99	$8.50	-	Oct-08 15:41
	Plate & Pot Wall Rack New		$20.99 $22.99	$18.65	-	Oct-08 15:30

Preview in a window

Get your listing seen by more buyers ②

Featured Plus ($19.95)
☐ Showcase your listing in the Featured area of search and listings. See example.

Gallery Featured ($19.95)
☐ Add a small version of your first picture to Search and Listings and showcase your picture in the Featured area of the Gallery view. See example.

Home Page Featured ($39.95)
☐ Get maximum exposure! Appear in our Featured area and your item is likely to appear on eBay's Home page. See example.

Review your listing ②

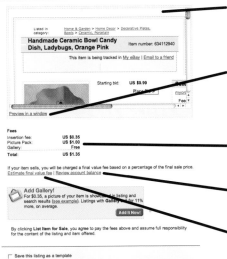

Listed in category: Home & Garden > Home Decor > Decorative Plates, Bowls > Ceramic, Porcelain
Handmade Ceramic Bowl Candy Dish, Ladybugs, Orange Pink   Item number: 634112940

This item is being tracked in My eBay | Email to a friend

Starting bid: US $9.99

Preview in a window

Fees
Insertion fee: US $0.35
Picture Pack: US $1.00
Gallery: Free
Total: **US $1.35**

If your item sells, you will be charged a final value fee based on a percentage of the final sale price.
Estimate final value fee | Review account balance

Add Gallery!
For $0.35, a picture of your item is showcased in listing and search results (see example). Listings with Gallery sell for 11% more, on average.   [Add It Now!]

By clicking List Item for Sale, you agree to pay the fees above and assume full responsibility for the content of the listing and item offered.

☐ Save this listing as a template
[List Item for Sale]

See what you'll get. The new Sell Your Item screens provide enhanced search-result and listing previews.

As you add listing upgrades, this area changes to show how your listing will appear in search-results pages— complete with other listings in the same category as yours.

View the preview in a separate window.

Scroll around in this window to preview and proofread your listing.

View your auction preview in a separate window.

Listing fees are summarized here.

Check your current eBay seller's account balance.

Click this link and the Help area displays eBay's Final Value Fee table.

Index